CASTLES
OF THE WESTERN WORLD

CASTLES
OF THE WESTERN WORLD

with 240 illustrations

ARMIN TUULSE

DOVER PUBLICATIONS, INC.
Mineola, New York

Bibliographical Note

This Dover edition, first published in 2002, is an unabridged republi-
cation of the work originally published in 1958 by Thames and Hudson,
London, which was, in turn, the English edition of the work published in
the same year by Anton Schroll and Co., Vienna. The book was translat-
ed from the German by R. P. Girdwood.

Library of Congress Cataloging-in-Publication Data

Tuulse, Armin.
    Castles of the Western world : with 240 illustrations / Armin Tuulse.
        p. cm.
    Originally published: London : Thames and Hudson, c1958.
    Includes bibliographical references (p.) and index.
    ISBN 0-486-42332-8 (pbk.)
        1. Castles—Europe. 2. Fortification—Europe. I. Title.

UG428 .T88 2002
728.8'1'094—dc21

2002067590

Manufactured in the United States of America
Dover Publications, Inc., 31 East 2nd Street, Mineola, N.Y. 11501

CONTENTS

PREHISTORIC TIMES AND ANTIQUITY
FROM EGYPT TO GREECE

The tower is a symbol of military architecture, the archetype of all the castles in the world. Man from time immemorial has set up towers of refuge and places of defence to give greater protection against the enemy than that provided by crude rock or stout tree. Remains of such fortresses are still to be seen in good condition even though they were built more than 3000 years before the birth of Christ. The turreted castle was already fully developed in the fortified royal residence at Abydos in Egypt. Contemporary sculpture and paintings of battle scenes provide further proof of this. Less elaborate were the fortresses in the border territories where they served as protection against both human and animal foes. There were similar towers also in Syria as can be seen from Egyptian sculptures at the beginning of the Syrian War in the Set epoch.

But there are other fortresses on the banks of the Nile which give indications of a further development. Cities were surrounded by a wall and the mighty Temple Citadels had defensive cordons provided with stout towers and gateways. A greater regularity marks both the sacred precincts and the palace of Rameses III at Medînet Habu (about 1200 B. C.). On both eastern and western sides there are massive gatehouses and the whole is surrounded by a double wall. The gateways are sited on the same axis and are small fortresses in themselves. This latter feature is evident in the design of other notable citadels of prehistoric times (ill. 1). This characteristic is even more marked in the preclassical military architecture of Mesopotamia where temple citadels with many walls and turrets grew to proportions which vied in their imposing size with natural mountain formations. First among these would be the Temple of Anu-Adads in Assyria, a sacred building remarkable for its Ziggurats or stepped pyramidal towers. Sargon's Palace in Khorsabad is a further example, as also is Babylon, the forerunner of all capital cities. All three have mighty walls with massive towers and imposing gateways. This was a lavish style of building which knew no shortage of material. An almost unlimited supply of manpower was available in the form of slave labour which performed feats of building that were not again possible until the present time with all its mechanical means of construction.

The Ishtar Gate in Babylon is particularly worthy of note (ill. 4). It was built about 600 B. C. and shows how much importance was attached in the ancient East to gateways, both from the practical as well as the symbolic point of view. These gateways were not only a gap in a defence system which therefore had to be heavily guarded but they also served a peaceful purpose in admitting normal traffic. It was here that the king used to meet his subjects who had to be impressed by his power and majesty. Ceremonial, in its most rigid form, always featured largely in the absolute theocratic monarchy of Babylon. The king was the representative of divine rule. The Ishtar Gate is a pre-eminent eastern example of fortress architecture with its system of multiple cordons which later was transformed and developed. But the Ishtar Gate is something more than this. It is a work of art. The flanking pillars of the gateway and the walls were decorated in bas-relief with symbols of sacred animals in glazed brickwork. These grimly menacing figures blend well with the massive style of the architecture.

The Temple Citadels of Mesopotamia are distinguished by the regularity of their ground plans. The solidity of walls and towers gives an impression of complete uniformity. Emphasis

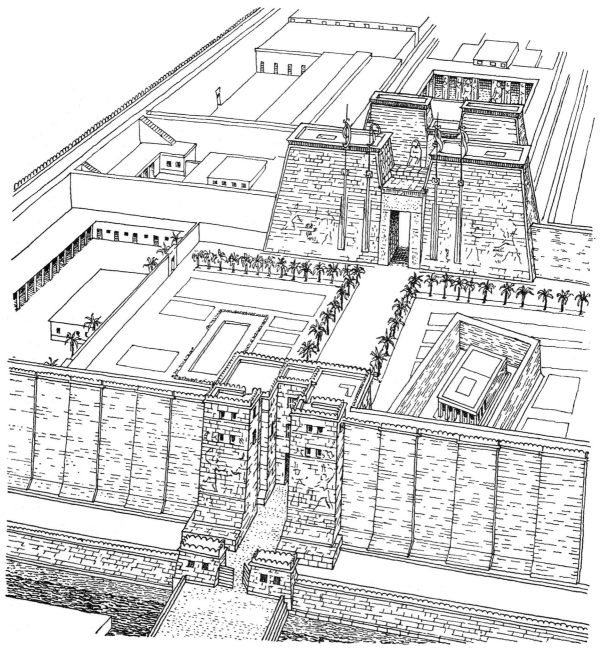

1 · Medinet Habu: reconstruction

2 · Sinjerli: reconstruction

is laid above all on passive defence. To achieve this the builders concentrated on height without working out the construction in detail. These features all show in unmistakable fashion the character of the old eastern military despotisms. Here, as in Egypt, the temple fortress occupied a specially favoured position in economic life. A vigorous trade flourished round the temple and the palace, and the whole industry of the country was centred outside the fortress walls.

The Hittites provided yet another example of the ancient eastern type of military architecture. They were a warlike people accustomed to rigid discipline although not so ferocious as the Assyrians.

The fortress of Sinjerli (10th—8th centuries B. C.) is one of the most remarkable military strongholds in the East (ill. 2). Here the ground plan is both oval and circular rather than austere and regular as favoured by the Egyptians and the inhabitants of Mesopotamia. The fortress is built on an eminence and the surrounding wall follows the contours of the ground. Even inside the fortress no attempt is made to follow any regular plans, for it is filled with several defensive cordons and so-called Hilani edifices, successors to the turreted castles mentioned above. The outer and inner city walls have semi-circular towers.

The whole city resembles in many details the medieval plan although the defence system was not so concentric as was usual later on in the West. At Sinjerli they have added one military building to another without co-ordinating them as a whole. The town, as such, surrounds the fortress with a double line of walls which boast a hundred towers and three gateways spaced at regular intervals.

A further example of this style of architecture is the Hittite city of Hathusa with its characteristic architectural details which recall a wooden wall. This suggests a certain contact with more Northern regions. The two types of ground plan, the strict and the more free, are already apparent in these early times and continue throughout the history of the citadel for more than 2000 years.

Troy, on its hill at Hissarlik, mythical Ilium, is a unique example of an ancient citadel. The site of nine different cities has clearly been established here. All indicate destruction by earthquake or by the hand of man. Over and over again the fortress has been rebuilt on the same spot. It is evident that the site was completely destroyed by a major catastrophe between 2300—2200 B. C. The walls which were built after this disaster follow a prescribed pattern which shows a point of concentration in the middle—a pattern quite alien to Mesopotamia and the ancient east as a whole. The sixth citadel was possibly that of Priam and a few of its foundations have been preserved in finely hewn blocks of stone. The entrance side is protected by three projecting four-sided towers. The actual entrance has no gateway of any great size but the road to the inside of the citadel goes along the city wall so that the garrison can repel the invaders from the top of the wall. The passive methods of defence of the ancient east are already beginning to be replaced by a more active defence system.

A new era dawned in citadel architecture with the beginning of the Minoan-Mycenean period. Direct influences from the East may be discovered in the oldest Cretan examples of military architecture, as for instance, the tower of ancient Knossos (about 2000 B. C.). The development in Crete later took on a peaceful character and the old tower disappeared beneath palace buildings which had no fortifications.

The citadels on the mainland are heavily fortified with huge walls. Mycene and Tiryns are classic examples. The fortress of Mycene is situated on an almost inaccessible mountain height (ill. 3) and its defence cordon consists of a wall of huge blocks of masonry, built to last for ever, a style of building attributed by the Greek to those giants of prehistoric times —the Cyclops. There is no trace of regularity in the surrounding wall. The character of the ground and the architecture itself have grown together into a new whole. The masterbuilder has made direct use of what the position of the fortress had to offer. From the fortification point of view Mycene betokens a diminution in size in comparison with the ancient fortresses of the east. Eastern passivity is now replaced by a vigorous activity. The powerful walls formed the only defence line of the fortress and on these walls, therefore, the decisive battle for the fate of the inhabitants of the fortress, their life, death or imprisonment, had to be waged. The foundation has grown out of several periods. Schliemann's excavations have shown that a primitive form of palace was first built on the spot in the 16th century B. C.

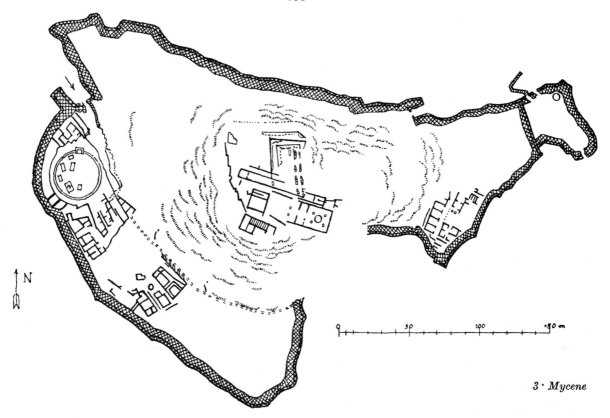

3 · Mycene

In the second half of the 14th century, a vast rebuilding of Mycene was undertaken, because of the increasing prosperity of the time. The ruler of Mycene at that period was a mighty prince, possibly from the famous house of Atreus. The greater part of the powerful "shell" walls, which still exist, were added at this time; the outer and inner parts were built of finely hewn blocks of stone and were more for outward appearance than for defensive purposes. The fortress had only one main entrance which was well protected by the wall. The well-known Lion Gate (ill. 5) belongs to this entrance and dates from the completion of the design of the fortress about 1250 B. C. The style here is quite different from that of Nebuchadnezzar's palace. Animals in stiffly ceremonial bas-relief accompanied those who entered the Ishtar Gate. At Mycene they were met by the emblem of a coat-of-arms, a veritable concentration of the means of expression. A theme borrowed from a skilled craft has been elaborated in a structurally modified form. The heads of the lion figures do not exist any more, but traces on the stone show that they might have been made of another material, probably metal.

The citadel of Tiryns was also developed through various building periods. Remains of an older city have been found, namely, a big round tower-like building in the middle of the courtyard of the fortress and this is thought to be where the prince lived. The interior was accessible through an entrance only to be reached by a ladder which could be taken away when danger threatened.

Directly after the completion of Mycene, Tiryns was also enlarged in the second half of the 14th century. The defensive system of Tiryns, like Mycene, is based on height and the walls follow the edges of the rock, although the lines are not so harshly shaped as in Mycene. The thick walls fit into one another and consist of huge irregular blocks of stone without mortar. The approach way is the only one to be specially protected and already suggests the manner in which it was always encountered in the Middle Ages.

The style of fortress of Mycene and Tiryns was reproduced in several other cities on the Greek mainland. A similar fortress existed on the Acropolis in Athens. A stretch of about 65 feet of its colossal Pelasgian Wall, south of Propylaeum, is still to be seen. All these fortresses were erected or completed in the second half of the 14th century when the Mycenean world, in its new feudal way of life, went through a dazzling period with new political constellations of power. Although the influence of these dynasties rasted on their material prosperity it was not the palace, as might be expected, but the fortress and the dome-shaped vault which were the monumental forms of expression.

The main task of the fortresses was undoubtedly to ensure the predominance of the dynasty in any possible wars. The fortresses previously described were destroyed as a consequence of the Doric immigration, a fate which had already threatened them in the 13th century, and which had therefore necessitated a strengthening of the defence work by the princes on the citadels at Mycene, Tiryns and Athens.

Citadels like Mycene and Tiryns undoubtedly received a stimulus from the national citadels. What is new about them points, on the other hand, towards future development, even if it does not directly foreshadow the medieval circular fortress.

On the other hand the turreted fortress continued on the Greek mainland, on the Aegean Islands and in Asia Minor, and its chief duty was now positively established. The tower became an important element in the country's defence both as a watch tower and as a signalling point. It was usually rectangular and, as a protection for the watchmen against surprise attacks by the enemy, it was surrounded by a circular outer wall. The stretch of land between the sea and the fortress of Pergamon near Bergama was provided with a row of towers of this sort, which were situated at a suitable distance apart for signalling from one to the next. But towers were also built on country houses, as strongholds in which the owner's treasures where kept in safety and to which he himself hastened, if danger threatened— a characteristic feature of towers throughout the centuries.

ROMAN FORTRESSES

The military expansion of Rome led to a great flowering of the art of fortification which freed itself from the cultural and princely forms of representation and pursued a course dictated by military needs.

The Romans sited their fortresses mainly in the frontier territories and all building was directed by the state. These edifices were spread over the whole Mediterranean area, now united under Roman rule, in a strongly-marked and unified style, and Northern Europe also for the first time fell into line with the principles of form laid down by the South.

Great as Roman achievements in fortress-building may have been, even here the development as usual was based on the practical knowledge and experience of the period. But the

4 · Babylon: Ishtar Gate
(Berlin, Staatliches Museum)

5 · Mycene: Gate of the Lions

6 · *Autun, France: Temple of Janus*

7 · *Rome: town wall of Aurelius*

originals were now entirely remodelled and adapted to suit the new requirements. When the turreted citadel—that archetype of fortress architecture—was adopted, the Eastern style was abandoned. This type of fortress played a leading part in Roman times and followed the legions throughout the Empire. The Romans, like the Greeks, employed the tower ultimately as a watch tower; the turreted fortress too probably reached the West by way of Greece. In their various forms one tower led to another all along the imperial boundaries in Europe, Africa and Asia. The towers of the German *limes* (the fortified frontier) were of the simplest type. If the frontier was protected by a moat, rampart and stockade, this defence line was usually guarded by square watch towers (*specula*) with walls 12 or 15 feet thick. These towers were originally of wood, and later of stone with a wooden superstructure. Towers of this sort are depicted in relief on the Trajan column in Rome. On stretches of fortified frontier without ramparts, frontier protection consisted only of isolated tower-like structures which were however larger than the rampart towers.

Towers with an area of 120 square yards are a standard type and correspond closely to the shape of the Greek watch towers. For the first time, under Antoninus Pius, a turreted fortress of this type is called a *burgus* (fortress). Wall foundations have been discovered by the more important waterways and highways, at trading centres and strategically important frontiers. At a later date, towers at important centres grew in size and appearance and fulfilled wider functions than those of a mere advance post or small fort. The Temple of Janus near Autun in France (ill. 6) can be regarded as one of these larger towers. It is a massive edifice which clearly indicates the development to come in the Middle Ages. The Tour Magne at Nimes is another example. There are also remains of larger *burgi* at Eisenberg near Grünstadt (Palatinate) and at Harlach near Weissenburg in Bavaria.

The enlarged *burgi* nevertheless had their beginning and their greatest expansion on the boundary between Africa and Arabia. It was in Africa above all that the simple, massive tower formation evolved into a real tower for living purposes with a more fully developed design. Ksar Tarcine (Tibubuci) in Tripoli has, in the middle of a polygonal city wall, a tower of 270 square yards in which the most noteworthy detail of the ground plan is a small court-yard or shaft to admit the light (ill. 8). There are several examples of this line of development in Africa, not only in Roman fortress buildings but also in private houses.

El Guercinet (*Turris Maniliorum*) is an oft-quoted monument which recalls the 'Atrium Houses' at Pompeii. Carl Schuchhardt assumes that these Africans *burgi* are connected with a surviving Egyptian tradition, as it is known that the fortified house for the upper classes was fairly usual. *Burgi* of a somewhat similar type to those in Tripoli were built on the Arabian frontier. In these also the courtyard was narrow in the early examples, in fact almost covered over, so that the door had to be used as a source of light (Râs el-Mušêrife, ill. 9).

The courtyard soon grew and the whole plan assumed larger dimensions until the *burgus* with the courtyard in the middle can no longer be designated as a tower. The transition from the house with a courtyard to the composite design, in a pronouncedly regular pattern, is seen most clearly in Syria where the European art of fortress construction later found new inspiration. Side by side with turret and fortress, another type of fortification was beginning to appear. This was the castle. *Castellum* was a diminutive of *castrum*, and must have meant a closed place of a smaller sort. But *castellum* was being used in a very vague sense, as was also *castrum*, although Caesar used this term for the national fortresses in Gaul. A regular quadrilateral ground plan is a characteristic of the Roman castle, and its defences consists of a surrounding wall, towers, ramparts and moats. Both western and eastern influences could be discovered in the combination of these essential components and in the inner buildings also. The same was the case with the turreted fortresses.

The classic example of the western line is the *castellum* of Saalburg near Homburg. An even better example of the European castle, from the point of view of military buildings, is Unterböbingen (ill. 10). A camp area of considerable circumference was surrounded by a regularly planned wall with rounded corners. The wall was breached by four symmetrically co-ordinated gateways which were protected by two four-sided towers situated on the inside of the wall. In the middle of the castle was the *praetorium*, which was also rectangular. The other castles in the European part of the Roman Empire were more or less similar in shape and all were marked by a strong regularity of design.

Special features like the rounded corners, and towers situated on the inner side of the wall, are often to be found, just as the grouping together of the houses in the middle of the courtyard is a characteristic of the development of the castle in the west.

The eastern *castellum* is quite different. A row of castles dating from the 2nd to the 4th centuries is to be found in Syria between Damascus and Hauran. These were all built after the same pattern (Kasr il abjad, ill. 11). The general design here was regular, as it was in Europe. The line of the walls is, however, in contrast with the early European castle in that it is provided with projecting corner towers, and the houses are grouped together around the inner wall. Instead of the usual four entrances there is only one. Castles are to be found with

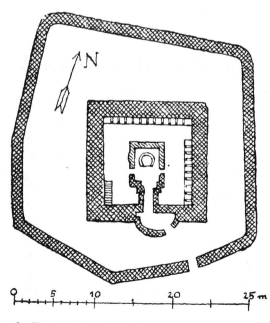

8 · *Ksar Tarcine, Tripoli: dwelling tower*

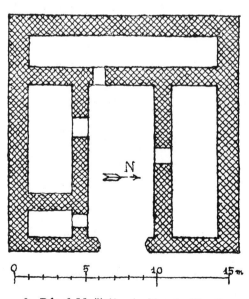

9 · *Râs el-Mušêrife, Arabia: dwelling tower*

rectangular flanking towers at the corners, which, with the grouping together of their houses round the courtyard, correspond closely with the enlarged *burgus* type (Kasr Bcher).

Special features are also encountered in Roman castles in Tripoli, which partly resemble the Syrian although they are not always so consistently carried out. In the eastern desert lands between Damascus and Hauran the castle was built for individual defence and consequently having the character rather of a permanently inhabited fortress. Moreover, in these areas the enemy's methods of attack were different from those of the north and traditions of the passive defence system of the ancient east partly lingered on, a state of affairs which must have had a pronounced effect on Roman building activity, as, indeed, it had on the turreted fortress at Tripoli. The existing material therefore shows clearly different phases of development in Roman fortress building as the frontier castle of early times is transformed into a small establishment, similar to a fortress, the *castella*.

The Arabs pursued this line of development from the 5th to the 8th centuries. Mshatta is the best known, but it was never completed and did not incorporate the fortress type of the Ummayads so clearly as Al Harani in Moab (before 710 A. D.) or Djebel Seis (ill. 12). The designs in question conform as much with the castle as with the enlarged *burgi*. The grouping of the houses in the interior is so homogeneous that they appear to be more closely related to the type of house with a courtyard than to a castle.

Byzantium, however, was the real successor to the Roman art of fortification and there is evidence of many fortress buildings and city walls.

In Byzantium the castle and projecting towers were handed down almost unchanged from one generation to another. The round or semi-circular tower was never able to make much headway in Byzantium, for preference was always given to the quadrilateral tower.

Western Europe, in the late Roman era, also made contact with the eastern development trends of the castle. The castles of Irgenhausen in Switzerland and Altrip near Ludwigshafen on the Rhine are worthy of note—and in comparison with these examples the effect produced

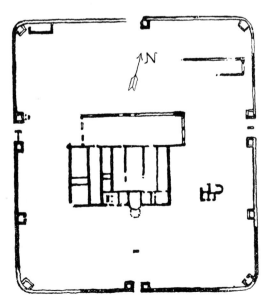

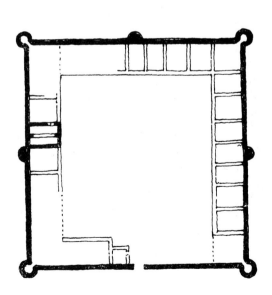

10 · Unterböbingen, Suabia: Roman castle   *11 · Kasr il abjad, Syria: Roman castle*

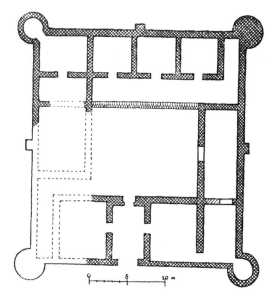

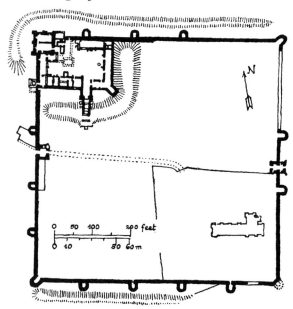

12 · Djebel Seis, Syria: Omayad fortress   *13 · Porchester, Hampshire: Roman castle and Norman fortress*

by the earlier designs of the Saalburg type appear very weak from the fortification point of view. Porchester, in Hampshire, is a well known edifice of this type with its semi-circular towers. It is built on the site of a prehistoric castle, the successor of which later became a Romanesque fortress (ill. 13). A similar development is obvious in the permanent defence design in the form of city walls. The mighty defence cordon of Rome is pre-eminent and was founded and completed in the 270 years between the reign of the Emperor Aurelian and the beginning of the 4th century (ill. 7). The flanking towers and the gateways flanked by turrets are here in their ultimate form. In Trier's Porta Nigra, the round tower appears in monumental guise. Diocletian's palace at Spalato (Split) in Dalmatia (Yugoslavia) is a fine example of the mingling of castle, fortress and villa. The clear cut symmetry of the Romans with hints of eastern influence are the predominating theme in this instance.

Alongside the military design of greater importance there existed innumerable smaller buildings of a more or less clearly defined military character. Roman colonists in the conquered territories must always have had to reckon with hostile invasions, so that even country villas, with their symmetrical, attractive housefronts and shady gardens, could not afford to ignore defence measures. On the whole these villas were situated in isolated spots in the open country and were exposed to every attack in times of uncertainty. As had been the case in earlier times with Greek farm buildings, the tower was also introduced here as a strong point and was either incorporated in the projection at the corner of the façade or used as a household building concealed at the back of the courtyard. The more uncertain the times, the more important was the part played by the tower in courtyard architecture. Remains of buildings are to be found in France as well as in Germany which testify to the increased significance of defence even of the isolated house up to the Merovingian era. Many buildings stubbornly retained their open and unprotected out-houses until the Middle Ages did away decisively even with these so as to unite military and domestic purposes in a totally new way. In this coming development the rural villa was to play a not insignificant part beside the castle and the *burgus*. Once more the chain of circumstances is revealed in which the castle, after the Middle Ages, extends its sphere exactly as in the period of late antiquity.

The Roman military edifice is recognised as the magnificent final chapter of the prehistoric and ancient development and at the same time a starting point and prototype for future ages. The strict regularity which marked Roman fortress building can be compared most nearly with that of Egypt and Mesopotamia. A connection between Imperial Rome and the ancient East is indicated in the southern provinces. At the same time the expansion of the tower and the lay-out of the castle are to be noted. A comparison between the military buildings in Rome on the one hand, and Mesopotamia and Egypt on the other, however, shows that the differences are more important than the similarities. In contrast with the concentrated sacerdotal effect of the ancient East, the Roman art of fortress building is marked by a functional realism, both tough and elastic, which could be likened to the contrast between the Babylonian bearded priests, numbed with ceremonial, and the valorous Roman praetorians. Even if military architecture finally depends on a number of practical factors—above all on methods of warfare and economic resources—the artistic style of the period is reflected in the form that it takes. The new spirit first dawned in Greece where the idea of the ancient Eastern wall was questioned because passive defence was combined with a more active system. The individual effort of individual men takes the place of masses of battlements, and the focal point of monumental sacred edifices now appears in the essentially symmetrical Grecian architecture. This symmetry is quite different from that of the East and bears the same relation to the Eastern sacred buildings as the Roman castle did to the defence cordons of the sacred citadels.

THE ROMANESQUE CASTLE

CAROLINGIAN

After the break up of the Roman Empire several hundred years were to elapse before a firmly organised building activity could take place. Century after century passed away. Christianity spread north of the Alps. A few remains of sacred buildings of the period are to be found here and there but one looks in vain for military building worthy of the name. People had to be content with refuge forts, entrenched themselves in ancient building monuments or, as was usually the case, did battle with their enemies under the open sky.

Nothing new appeared in the development of the art of secular building until the reign of Charlemagne (768—814). It then revealed itself as a peculiar mixture more like an arbitrary union of very diverse elements than a really new creation. The medieval fortress was not yet fully developed, but the final form began to be foreshadowed and some of the chief constituents were starting to evolve. The changed political and economic circumstances led to demands for fuller and more pretentious living conditions. A well ordered national life replaced the long period of warfare and uncertainty. Foreign enemies, such as the

Arabs, Avars and Slavs, were repulsed at the frontiers and there was unity in the country itself. A new central force made itself felt, not only political but also cultural.

A brilliant court life took shape, clearly modelled on that of Rome and Byzantium. The imperial palace arose as the symbol of the new power. At his coronation in 800 Charlemagne could well regard himself, with his Frankish Kingdom, as the successor to the mighty Roman emperors and in his government buildings, consciously imitated those of his Roman predecessors. In this he resembled earlier German monarchs, like Theoderic, whose Palatium at Ravenna gets its name from the Palatine in Rome, where Augustus had lived. For more than a thousand years after that time the name Palace, Palatium, Palazzo, Palast was a synonym for the distinguished and the splendid in domestic architecture. But an emperor's palace was not a fortress, nor a strong point, but only the chief place for political negotiations and a symbol of the imperial jurisdiction. None of the many Carolingian palaces can be put down as the chief residence of the emperors even if certain claims to be the capital are not easily denied. According to ancient custom, the court usually went from palace to palace and because of the strongly defined agrarian system of the period the palaces were built in country areas, for a distant attitude towards the cities still prevailed. The old Roman buildings had fallen into decay or their material had been utilised for new buildings, as happened under Charlemagne when in the last quarter of the 8th century he expanded and improved Aachen because of its new claims to be represented. The material was taken from, amongst other places, those Roman imperial cities rich in tradition, Arles, Trier and Ravenna. Only the chapel, the famous cathedral, a polygonal centrally planned building of Byzantine design with unique characteristics, remains. The chapel was consecrated in 805, by which time a whole row of other buildings were ready in the spacious block. Through this building activity the old Merovingian imperial court maintained a regularity which shows a clear connection with the late Roman palaces. Pippin's palace building (*regia*) was linked with the chapel, by a long corridor, in the middle of which there was a portico. In this way a group of buildings originated which was later the model for royal palaces and survived stubbornly until the palace became assimilated with the citadel, and the narrow courtyard of this relic of late antiquity was destroyed. Aachen had no defence buildings of any kind under Charlemagne if one excepts the Grannus Tower on the eastern side of the palace building. Its age cannot be determined.

The royal palace in Ingelheim could well have vied with the great palaces in Byzantium and Rome both in its size and artistic shape (ill. 14). This palace was also started by Charlemagne but it was not completed until 819 in the reign of Louis the Pious. In this instance the buildings are grouped together in a rectangle where inner courtyards are encircled by pillared galleries as in Roman villas. The principal buildings have the shape of a basilica and a big hall is joined on to the eastern side. There are several elements in the design which recall Mshatta and Al Harani as well as Diocletian's palace at Split, although the lay-out as a whole is very different from these. Ingelheim was not a coordinated warlike block of buildings; its architectural features lay exposed to the peaceful countryside. The reconstruction does not resolve all the difficulties, but it is certain that the lay-out

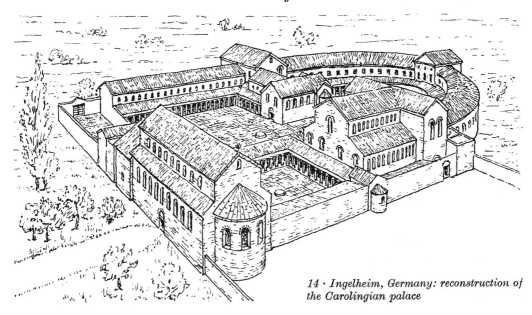

*14 · Ingelheim, Germany: reconstruction of
the Carolingian palace*

conforms to late Roman, rather than to German, traditions. It is still a matter for conjecture
to what extent Ingelheim can trace its descent directly from buildings in Constantinople,
Split, the Palatine in Rome or the palace in Ravenna. Ingelheim, also, like Aachen, had no
special defence arrangements at the time of Charlemagne. The undivided power of the
emperor as well as the inner stability of the Empire made permanent protection unnecessary.
In emergencies the royal retinue had to band together round the Emperor like a living wall,
in the traditional way.

A different state of affairs existed in the smaller royal households which in the Carolingian
period were established in great numbers, and which were usually fortified. The Franks
revealed themselves as direct successors of the Romans in their wars with the Saxons.
Frankish citadels were planned in connection with the old Saxon popular fortresses and
domains, for the subjection and economic exploitation of the conquered Saxon territories.
It was necessary, moreover, to build fortified royal residences (*curtes regiae*) at the more
important road junctions. These residences, as reinforcement bases, had the task of ensuring
peaceful traffic. Some of these later fortifications might, it was thought, have originated
in Roman times, but excavations have proved that they are of the Carolingian period.
In fact both ground plan and style of building of these royal palaces have several features
which are characteristic of the Roman castle.

The main fortress is usually square in shape with rounded-off corners and generally has no
turrets. The changed circumstances of the times were indeed a reason for this in that the
size was now considerably less than the Roman *limes* castles—mostly 110 yards square,
a size which was exceeded by even the smallest Roman military fortress. It should also be
noted the Roman foot was used as unit of measurement in building these fortresses. Rampart
and moat were connected to the surrounding wall as at the Saalburg near Homburg. The
main fortress was protected by an advance post which in most cases is of irregular shape.

A lay-out of this type is exemplified by the Heisterburg at Deister (ill. 15). The main
fortress had to ensure the safety of the harvest and to supply passing troops with stores.
The advance fort was used as a camp for the troops. The houses in the main fortress are not
grouped together and there is no dominating central building. This was due to the fact
that a visit from the monarch was not expected. Quite a different state of affairs existed
in the larger royal castles like Dorestad in Holland where the lay-out consisted of a rear
part (*curtis*), a forward part (*curticula*) and an advanced fort (*pomerium*). A building
rectangular in shape, measuring 50 feet by 65 feet, similar to a Roman *praetorium*, stood
in the middle of the *curtis*. It is known from descriptions of royal palaces that this house
served as a residence for the ruler if he visited the place and that for this reason it was
named the *sala regalis* or *domus regalis*.

The castle-citadels of the Franks are only encountered in western Lower Saxony, where
there was fierce resistance. The circular fortress is the predominating type in eastern Saxony
between Weser and Elbe. The old north European tradition survived here even after the
country's subjection, and the citadels which were built in Charlemagne's time for the
government of the country were characterised by their defensive main parts. The best
known of these Saxon citadels is the Pipinsburg near Geestemünde (ill. 16) which was
protected by an enormously thick rampart with a moat. This is of considerable width in
comparison with other Frankish moats which are deeper in the middle after the Roman
fashion. When one sees the grouping of the buildings in the courtyard of the citadel even
greater differences from the Frankish castle are apparent. The place of the *sala regalis* in
the middle of the courtyard remains empty and, instead, almost equally large buildings
round the courtyard seek protection in the shadow of the rampart. This is a special feature
which was reproduced in the later development.

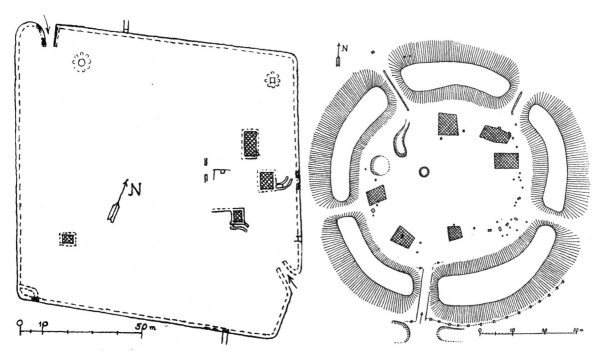

15 · Heisterburg, Germany: Frankish fortress   *16 · Pipinsburg, Germany: Saxon fortress*

It would be incorrect to apply too comprehensive a generalisation. In the Middle Ages the hill-fort with its ramparts and the castle in different localities play a large role beside the tower, and preference was given to one or the other type according to the economic, social and military background. What probably occurred, most frequently however, was that the various components were combined with one another.

NORMAN

Building activity under Charlemagne was ordered principally by the monarch himself and those nearest him in the court and Church. There was no broader basis. When the country was later split up and the rigid order was relaxed in places, internal unrest broke out and enemy attacks were threatened from beyond the borders of the kingdom. This put an end to all prospects of further building which had started off so hopefully. Even in fortress architecture the eastern part of the Frankish kingdom was, in the following centuries, marked by a conservative trend. And in Francia Occidentalis, devastated by the Norse both on the coast and in the interior, conditions in the 9th and 10th centuries were hardly any better. The prayer 'A furore Normannorum libera nos Domine' sounded throughout the Churches. But the Norse peril had a stimulating effect on the development of military building. Even in 864 Charles the Bald had firmly forbidden all private building of fortresses without special permission. But it soon appeared that the royal power was helpless when up against the Norse raids and consequently the veto of 864 was revoked in the following manner. The nobles obtained permission to build fortresses on their own property for the purpose of giving both themselves and their dependents a better protection against the invaders. The gateway was consequently developed to a great extent and this led to monumental creations in the fortress architecture of the western world. It later became the invaders' turn to take over the lead in promoting a flourishing architectural system. After the Viking Rollo had married a Carolingian wife and the whole coast-line of Neustria (later to be called Normandy) had been subjected, Norse activity was no longer centred on predatory raids but rather on the building of fortresses. The proud and mighty Norman fortress did not spring full-grown, however, like Athena out of the head of Zeus. Remains of the earliest Norman fortresses lie hidden for the most part, under the ground. But the archaeologists' spade has brought to light sufficient material for reconstructing the oldest plans in their original condition. The excavations carried out at Caumont particularly, have made clear the beginnings of the Norman fortress. The oldest type consisted of a turreted fortress which was erected either on the natural slope of the ground or on an artificially created hill (*motte*) which can often assume great dimensions. These towers were originally built mainly of wood and were at first used as occasional places of refuge. For purposes of everyday life there were dwelling houses and farm buildings next to the tower, which were mostly protected by a moat and stockades. The fortress did not always stand alone on its hill but a small type of advance fort was connected to it rather in the manner of the *curtis* and *curticula* in the royal palaces of the Frankish rulers. Hills of this sort, surmounted by a tower, rapidly increased in number and, apart from Normandy, there are particularly fine examples in England, and also in Germany and Scandinavia. There are several early turreted fortresses on mottes which are depicted in the famous Bayeux Tapestry from the second half of the eleventh century.

One should not reject out of hand a possible connection between the motte lay-out with towers and the Roman turreted fortresses. The *limes* castle is usually named as the original and in point of fact both nearly approximated to it in their outward appearance. But the unbroken line of tradition goes through the country castle where the tower had always been a place of refuge, rather than through fortresses at the frontier. No special examples were needed to continue these old systems with one of the basic elements of fortress building, namely defence through height.

The mighty hills, artificially created for defence purposes, are not always provided with towers and there are even some which had only a stockade wall, circular in shape, on the upper platform of the hill, a special feature which has likewise contributed to later development. The Norman turreted fortress illustrates nevertheless the growth of feudal conditions and the flourishing of the knightly life of the Middle Ages. The temporary towers of refuge grew quickly in number and size. They now not only fulfilled their task of protection against the Vikings but were also used by their ruler in his lust for power. The tower was suited to the needs of daily life and its military and domestic purposes were united. Thus the medieval fortress as a complete creation stands before us. Individual military units grow up and spread quickly over the west, replacing the Roman and Carolingian fortress camps which like the prehistoric citadels had the task of collective defence. Nearly 40,000 strongholds were erected in France alone during the Middle Ages. The knight stands forth as the creator of this new world with his worship of Mary, his fight against the infidels and the protection of the weak as devices on his banner. A new social group, the most exclusive there has ever been, emerged and formed a select, social phenomenon within the state, separated from everything that was simple and ordinary. The duty of drawing the sword for Christ raised the conduct of fighting out of its essential brutality and made it into a noble art. The ideal and romantic veneration for women united valour in battle with the romantic life of song, music and dance.

A more broad and highly promising way was opened for the development of fortress building through this combination of the contemporary exigencies of defence and the social pattern of the knightly way of life.

Chief emphasis was laid at the beginning on defence and the early feudal fortress was built up in a highly significant manner on Norman soil. Wood was for a long time the main material of construction but this did not prevent the buildings from attaining considerable size and adequate effectiveness. The character of the turreted fortress was already fully developed when stone was first employed as building material after the dark ages at the end of the first millenium A. D. Military architecture played a large part in the development of the Norman-Romanesque building art. Mighty turreted fortresses were erected, the shapes of which clearly reflected the universal joy of creation of the period and the will of the sovereign. Even the nomenclature is characteristic: donjon—from the Low Latin *dominatio*

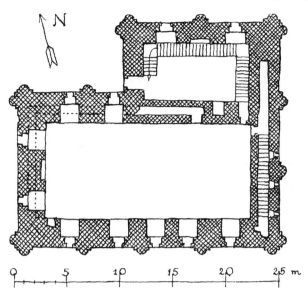

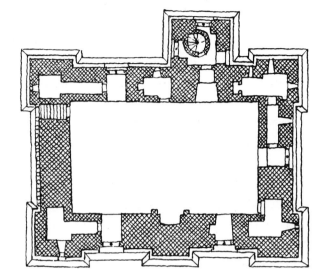

17 · *Loches, France: donjon*

18 · *Chambois, France: donjon*

(sovereignty). The first keeps were in existence about the year 1000, when the basic elements of the Romanesque style were almost completed. The custom of building walls of squared stone is adopted once more, and a new monumentality is demonstrated which is distinguished by a robust strength with a strong new creative tendency, quite different from the mechanical combination of different elements in the Carolingian period. The keeps maintained a fairly uniform appearance for they were dependent on similar internal and external circumstances as well as on the rapid rate of development. A uniformity prevailed which is peculiar to times in which either great leading ideas or certain social characteristics and assumptions are at work.

Langeais (992) should be considered as the oldest keep; however this does not mean that tower building at this date was already fully developed. This keep is a rather broad, somewhat longish four-cornered tower with projecting buttresses on the outer walls. There is an oft-quoted example at Loches dating from the eleventh century (ill. 17, 22).

The division of the rooms inside is simple and reminds one of the traditions of building in wood of earlier centuries. The upper storeys were arranged as living rooms but the chief emphasis is still always laid on defence, a feature which is also predominant among other keeps of this period. The semi-circular pilaster-strips are in accordance with the sacred architecture of the time such as the Church of Mont St. Michel. The pilaster-strips in Niort (about 1160) already appear in the form of small turrets (ill. 23). The lay-out consists of two rectangular keeps which are connected by a central building which, in the late Middle Ages, was turned into a dwelling house. Chambois (Orne) represents the ultimate phase of development of the rectangular keep. There the corner

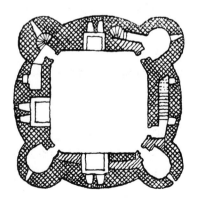

19 · *Houdan, France: donjon*

pilaster-strips reached their full growth as four-cornered turrets (ill. 18). Their turrets, however, were not designed for protecting the flanks, that is the tower could not be defended
from the corners with lateral fire. Defence was still always vertical and frontal in form.
Chambois, like Loches, had a small well for a staircase. The first floor consisted of a large
hall with beautiful and unusually large window-openings as well as a chimney. Here is to
be found one of the first French halls of the Knights, a forerunner of the artistic
interiors of the Gothic period. The desire for more light and more air began to break
through the massive walls in the first century of the keep's history.

The shape of the keep in the late Romanesque period becomes more and more modified
and a clear connection can often be traced with religious architecture. Early forms and
wooden buildings disappear and the high Romanesque style, the combination of cubic and
cylindrical forms, becomes more and more clear-cut. The improvement in the technical art
of the arch causes the circular ground plan to be often preferred. The rooms in Houdan
(completed 1137—ill. 19) are still rectangular while the outside of the tower is round, whereby
the four powerful corner turrets approximate more closely in appearance to a rectangle.

The octagonal keep at Provins (Tour de César) dating from the middle of the twelfth century
has a striking appearance owing to the turrets at the corners (ill. 21). The keep at Etampes

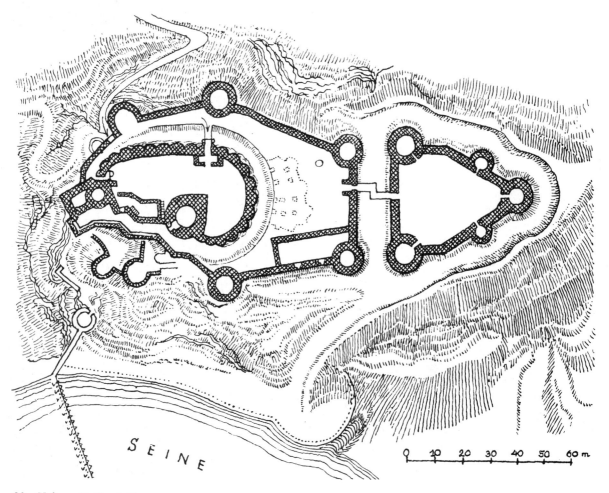

20 · *Château Gaillard, France*

21 · *Provins, France: Tour de César*

22 · *Loches, France: donjon*

23 · Niort, France: donjons

24 · Château Gaillard, France

25 · London: White Tower

26 · London: Chapel of St John, in the White Tower

27 · Rising: staircase of the keep

28 · *Hedingham: keep*

29 · *Restormel, Cornwall: shell keep*

30 · *Palermo, Sicily: La Cuba*

31 · *San Gimignano, Italy: family towers*

(about 1140) is a highly original variation of the keep at Houdan for it is made up of four semi-circular towers.

Richard Coeur de Lion's enormous Château Gaillard on the Seine, completed in 1198, is one of the last in the succession of Romanesque keeps. The central part of the fortress dates from this period. It has a massive tower and surrounding wall adapted to the lie of the land (ill. 20, 24). The main tower had developed after the fortress into a wedge-shaped salient and the upper part has buttresses arranged in sloping fashion. These possibly had to support a path for the defenders with projecting loopholes on the upper platform tower, now in ruins. If this was really the case we here come across the first loopholes in the west of the Mashikuli type, which did not reach their fullest extent until much later.

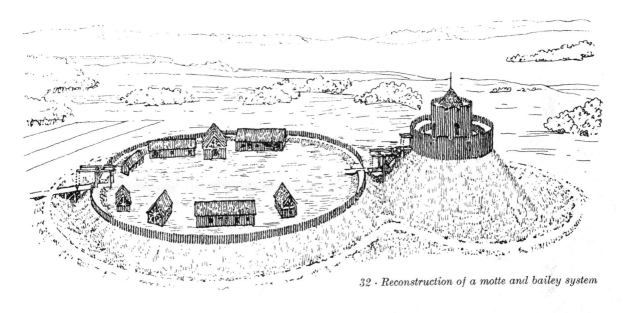

32 · *Reconstruction of a motte and bailey system*

The tower was almost entirely for defensive purposes and had no domestic arrangements. The houses for everyday requirements are on the inner side of the circular wall. The older type of keep here relinquishes its position as sole master of the whole design, with varying styles of building. The circular wall of the older part is characteristic with its semi-circular protrusions like small turrets which are situated close to each other. The wall serves in this way as a screen of strong planking and from afar is reminiscent of the wooden fortresses. The outer cordon of walls is in sharp contrast with this older part for it is laid out in straight lines with flanking towers. This part dates from the beginning of the 13th century and already indicates a later way of development.

After the battle of Hastings in 1066 fortress architecture in England also began to flourish vigorously. William I and his supporters were largely responsible for this so as to strengthen their position in the vanquished territory. The new monarch strove to centralise his own power in spite of the introduction of the feudal system.

A great number of castles therefore arose—there are more than 100 dated earlier than 1100—and it is probable that the number is even higher. Most of these buildings have now vanished and were for certain built of wood. The motte plan, already tested in Normandy, was used in which a tower or a stockade wall was erected (ill. 32).

There are several hundred places of this type in the British Isles, especially numerous in Wales, but they were also introduced into Scotland at the beginning of the twelfth century and into Ireland at the time of the Anglo-Norman invasion in the last quarter of the twelfth century. The most important of these early fortresses were incorporated into later buildings of stone, in which during a long transition period a building style combining wood and stone is employed. Stone buildings began to be erected even in the time of William the Conqueror. Several mighty works—defiant towers of a kind similar to those in Normandy—were built by the new rulers and they were a great economic source of help to them in the recently subjugated country which stood at their disposal. The donjon, the symbol of might and supremacy became also in England the chief type of fortress, although in this case it was usually given the name of 'keep'. While fortresses were still in use they were in general called 'Towers'.

The well-known Tower of London (White Tower) was founded about 1070 under William I and was completed in the 1090's (ill. 25, 33). The cube-shaped building with its many pilasters and narrow corner towers is typically Norman.

Nevertheless it is not a direct copy of the French donjon as, in contrast with the French lay-out of the rooms, it contains several elements, namely living-rooms, hall and chapel, which are concentrated in a single design. St. John's Chapel (ill. 26) dominates a special part of the edifice and juts out of the heavy mass of the cube. It can be deduced from the ground plan alone that in this instance it was a question of adapting the building to other forms of life with greater claims to be represented and a much stronger economic

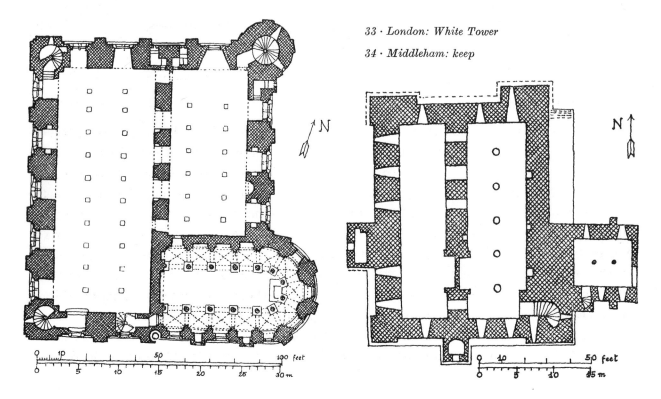

33 · *London: White Tower*

34 · *Middleham: keep*

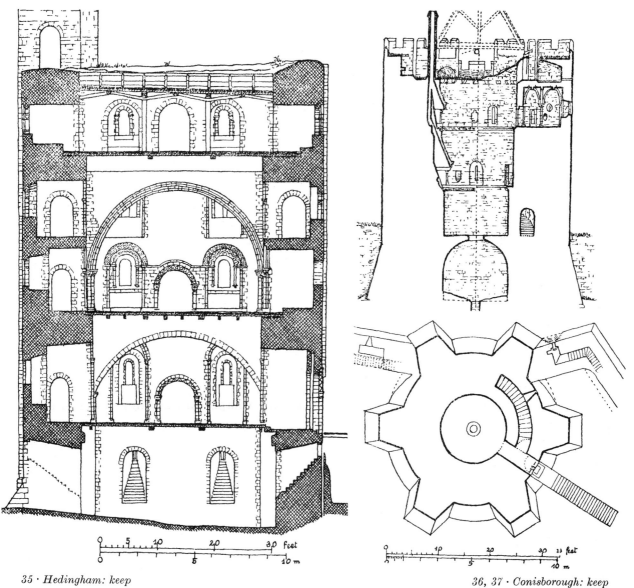

35 · *Hedingham: keep*

36, 37 · *Conisborough: keep*

background than existed at that time in William I's homeland. A similar solution, but on a far larger scale, is encountered at Colchester in Essex (about 1090). Here the large rooms are grouped round the typical English hall. All demands for comfort necessary in a palace-like building have been satisfied without, at the same time, ignoring the need for fortification. The Great Hall and the apartments in turreted fortresses of this type are situated mostly next to one another on the same storey, for which reason the shape of the turret was both broad and low, a so-called 'Hall Keep'. The keeps in London and Colchester are the only ones which date from the 11th century but a similar ground plan is encountered later (e. g. Middleham in Yorkshire, about 1170). Here there is a perfect merging of military and palatial building in the same proportion (ill. 34). The tower has frequently a special gate-house building; the flight of stairs usually leads straight into the hall which, more than anything else, became the main setting for the life of the knights. The mighty feudal lord presided in the hall over his guests, his retinue and the whole of his household. There solemn ceremonies were enacted, there justice was dispensed, and there they used to gather for the meal. Both hall and gate-house building are often distinguished by their strongly marked Norman shape (Rising, ill. 27).

A great number of keeps were built in the 12th century which, in their lofty form, outwardly are reminiscent at times of the Norman keeps. One of the finest examples of this type is at Hedingham in Essex whose graceful corner towers can be compared with Chambois (ill. 28, 35). The division of the rooms also recalls French keeps. Rochester in Kent, begun in 1130, belongs to the same category.

The long reign of Henry II (1154—1189) marked a very important era in keep architecture, because he strove to unite the royal powers once more and to weaken the influence of the nobility. Scarborough was the first of a series of fortresses and then in 1171 Newcastle was built. This was a citadel with the typical four corner towers and a hall as a special feature. Henry II's last great keep was Dover, which was probably designed by a French architect who, nevertheless, to a great extent followed the traditions which had already developed early in England.

In Henry II's reign, polygonal and round keeps were also beginning to be built. The 12-sided keep at Oxford (1166—1170) should be considered as an original experiment with a new form. A very strong French influence is apparent in the keep at Conisborough (1180—1190) which is one of the first round keeps to have projecting buttresses (ill. 36, 37). Inside the towers the fortification is simple in style and it is only on the upper storey that the style is somewhat richer with a small chapel and heavy Norman cruciform arches. In Pembroke also there is a round keep of about 1200 which is considered to be the finest of its type in England. Pembroke, like Conisborough, is more akin to the building style of the Norman homeland than is the case with the rectangular towers. From the beginning of the 13th century onwards the round tower becomes more and more usual so that it finally becomes in the following decades part of the inside of the fortress and its flanking towers by means of a surrounding wall. Already in the early Norman period a special type of fortress is being developed in England, side by side with the rectangular, multilateral or round tower. This is the 'Shell Keep'. This is situated almost always on an old fortress-hill where the old stockade has been replaced quite simply by a stone wall. Shell keeps of this type were not generally used at the beginning as dwellings but rather as citadels or as a final place of withdrawal. Restormel (Cornwall) is a good example of such a citadel (ill. 29, 38). Other fine specimens are to be found at Carisbrooke (Isle of Wight) and Berkeley (Gloucestershire). The shell keeps at Windsor and Durham have been so much altered that they must be considered as new buildings.

The Anglo-Norman turreted fortress is the most notable new creation in the field of citadel-building from the standpoint of general development. Only the very earliest wooden turreted fortifications had a possible link with the Roman pattern. Those citadels which were built after the Dark Ages have just as little to do with the *limes* castle as the Norman cathedrals with the Roman basilica. The Romanesque sense of style found the same pronounced expression in donjon and keep as in the building of churches and it is difficult therefore to draw any clearly defined line of distinction between the sacred and the secular. It is certain that one and the same architect designed churches as well as fortifications and the form of churches had already taken shape when stonebuilt fortress-dwellings began to be introduced. The church tower often had a fortified appearance and it is known for certain that Irish campaniles served as towers of refuge in time of danger. Even the keep was originally only a tower which would suit just as well as a sacred building.

It was in England that a more distinctive form of turreted fortress first developed in which domestic purposes were strongly stressed. The emphasis on strength in this period is seen in the severe lines of the churches and the great halls with their Norman zig-zag ornamentation on massive arches, on the broad, monumental staircases and, last but not least, on the soaring turrets which reach up in a proud and self confident manner. All these are a visible expression of the unlimited opportunities which lay before the King and his high nobility

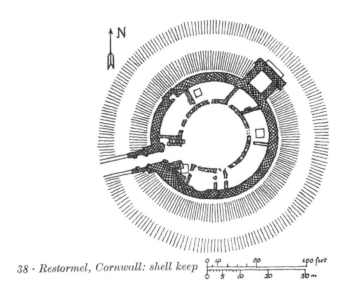

38 · *Restormel, Cornwall: shell keep*

after the Battle of Hastings. Donjon and keep grew up in clear forms which were not exclusively limited to defence purposes for which there were many solutions—but which have proved themselves symbols of the life of their period, symbols of which people of that time were only dimly aware.

The Normans had already invaded Southern Italy before they conquered England. The foundations of their power were laid in Salerno in 1061. Soon afterwards Calabria and the whole of Sicily were subjugated and already in 1081 Robert Guiscard was able to launch an attack on Constantinople. In 1130 the Norman King, Roger II, was crowned King of Sicily with great pomp in Palermo Cathedral. The Normans' great capacity for adaptation has already been shown by the development in Normandy and England. This led to new creations of great magnitude. In the cultural milieu of the Mediterranean, so strange for these Northern people, this impulse soon came to an end. The Normans encountered here an over-ruling Arabian influence which soon made its imprint on the Sicilian court and, already in the second generation, the successors of the Normans verged towards the people of the Orient in their customs and general way of life. This metamorphosis is illustrated best in the field of military building. Roger I (died 1101) was still a real Norman and his turreted fortress of Adernò in Sicily (ill. 39, 40) was a typical keep, the only difference being the sunny Mediterranean climate. The Northern construction with its projecting features is given up for cube-shaped building, calm and static in appearance. The lower, circular wall with semi-circular reinforced corners obviously belongs to a later date. Adernò corresponds very closely to the Tower of London in the division of its rooms. Chapel, living-room and hall are on the upper storey and here the chapel also has an apse which is however self-supporting, in contrast with the projecting choir in the tower inside the wall. The Normans also gave themselves in Adernò a feeling of home by the introduction of open fire-places, a very unusual feature in Italy.

There was a fusion in the 12th century between Norman and Arabian elements which is to be seen most clearly in the great palaces and castles which in a very short time (1130—1180) were erected in Palermo and the surrounding country. The most famous masterbuilder of the period was William II and both the cathedral and the monastery of Monreale are reckoned, with others, to rank with the immortal souvenirs of this reign. Buildings of great significance had already been erected by his predecessor, the hated William I, whom the chronicles depict as a cruel, bearded sultan, who at his death was mourned only by the Arabian women of his harem. It was he who had ordered the famous Zisa in Palermo to be built, originally called in Arabic 'El Aziz'—the beautiful—which, in spite of many alterations, is even now described as one of the finest sights to be seen in Palermo (ill. 41, 42).

Zisa is a turreted building which at first sight makes one think of Norman architecture; but on closer examination however the strong Arab elements are seen to predominate. The exterior is accordingly overlaid with archivolts in relief. These are in sharp contrast with the significantly vigorous forms of the façade in Norman-Gothic style. A high, wide portal with pointed Arab arches in the middle of the façade gives a palace-like appearance to the building. On passing through the entrance and going through a long hall one comes to a room two storeys high, still existing in the middle of the Tower. This room has a fountain and a real Arab stalactite cupola. Round this hall with the fountain the living rooms are grouped on two floors of strictly regular proportions. The third floor consists of a single room which in Alberti's time still had an opening in the middle of the ceiling. This last-named feature makes one think of the development of the Roman turreted fortress in Africa which resulted in the maturing of the enlarged *burgus* with its courtyard. We are standing therefore once more on the ground of Mediterranean culture, rich in tradition, with its long succession of turreted edifices beginning with the simple watch tower up to the galleried house (hilani) and the house with a courtyard.

The Cuba in Palermo is just like the Zisa in its construction, like a tower on a rectangular foundation. It appears to have been more of a banqueting hall than a palace for the central room is even bigger than in Zisa. The walls are decorated with niches studded with stalactites, and the roof had probably originally an opening in the middle—the indication of an inner

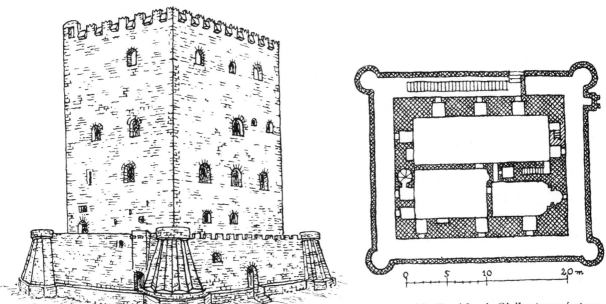

39, 40 · Adernò, Sicily: tower fortress

courtyard. There is no lack of Byzantine-Arabian characteristics of style. Even the calligraphic inscription of the façade is Arab. Zisa and Cuba were just like the parkland castles of Favara and Menani which were set in gardens with fountains and fishponds, and everything was welcomed here which the Arab style of living had to offer in the way of charm and intellectual stimulus. Christian and Muslim emblems were stamped with the same die (ill. 30).

The tower, as an individual defence point, appears relatively early also in central and northern Italy. This is a feature, however, which should not be attributed to the Norman turreted castle. The old tower tradition still persisted in many ways.

There is a remarkable story of Gregory of Tours according to which in about 581 a monk in the vicinity of Nice was held in a tower the entrance of which was not on a level with the ground; it was thus an early military tower. Turreted buildings in Italy became widespread under the Langobards who set them up as watch towers *(guardinghi)*. Towers were also built at a very early date in the coastal areas of the Roman campagna. These towers had to protect the population against the attacks of the Saracens *(torri saracinesche)*. Stone towers are heard of in cities from the eleventh century onwards and in the twelfth century these towers sprouted like mushrooms to the heavens, especially in the cities of Tuscany but also in other town communities. San Gimignano became famous for its thirteen towers of this kind (ill. 31). In Bologna there were two leaning towers as attractions for tourists, Asinelli and Garisenda. This city in the Middle Ages had at least 180 monuments of this type and Florence had over 200. Internal feuds of various kinds were the reason for the introduction of such towers. When the nobleman of the twelfth century went into the cities he had to make his defence measures fit in with the limited space at his disposal within the city walls. Consequently a slender tower was erected next to the house with which it was usually connected by a drawbridge and which served in times of trouble as the last place

41, 42 · *Palermo, Sicily: La Zisa*

of refuge. There was no entrance to the ground floor and the tower was erected entirely for defensive purposes.

These family towers or turret-shaped houses (*casatorri*) were inspired by the Norman donjon or keep according to their type. Their forerunners are to be found in Byzantium where the tower house was already widespread in the fifth century. The dominating Byzantine influence in Italy's artistic development in the first 1000 years after Christ can therefore be credited with the family tower as an immediate heir to Roman-Eastern traditions.

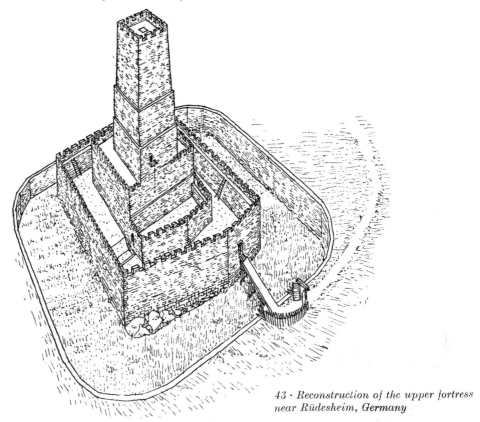

43 · Reconstruction of the upper fortress near Rüdesheim, Germany

TOWER, SURROUNDING WALL AND PALACE

The development of fortress architecture on German soil does not proceed so clearly in the first half of the Middle Ages as it did in Normandy and England. The halcyon period at the end of the first millennium A. D. did not begin so strikingly as in Western Europe, a circumstance which resulted in an obstinate survival of the old traditions. Henry I (916—936) probably sought to introduce fortresses and fortified towns as a protection against the Slavs and to repel the attacks of the Hungarians, but it is not entirely impossible that most towns, even in his time, were still protected by stockade, rampart and moat. As for the fortresses the national earthworks of the past still played a large part and the transition from these lay-outs with a military emphasis to the medieval fortress with its combination of military, domestic and economic uses proceeded very slowly. A long interim period must be reckoned with, in which ramparts and buildings of both wood and stone were built, in which the development of the various types was dependent, in the first place, on the form of the settlement and the growth of the large free-tenure system. Parallel with the greater extension of the feudal system in which the highest state officials received large tracts of land on loan from the princes, which they in turn let off to their vassals, the defence lay-outs of the olden type were more and more frequently replaced by privately owned fortresses.

The higher nobility from the 11th century onwards, used to take the name of castles as their family name and in the following century the lesser nobility began to do the same. The age-old, timeless elements of defence, tower and walls, were now grouped together. A new class arose in society with over ten thousand fortresses in German-speaking countries.

There were several patterns from which to choose. The turreted castle had maintained its existence continuously even in the German lands.

Nevertheless the medieval development here led meanwhile to a totally different type from that in Normandy. These differences are best studied in the Rhineland and in Alsace, where a reciprocal traffic between east and west resulted in a series of interesting turreted citadels. The Ober- and Niederburg near Rüdesheim are early examples in the Rhineland. They were founded in the first half of the 11th century. Both consist of a four-sided tower inside a surrounding wall. In comparison with western keeps these towers are narrower and only designed for defence, in which respect they prove to be connected with the early motte towers. This is especially so in the case of the Oberburg. There are also many turreted citadels in the Odenwald land (Breuberg, Lindenfels).

Steinsberg in Baden is a late example of a Romanesque tower which is constructed of squared stone with bosses on it (ill. 45, 46). A wall surrounds the eight-sided main tower and follows in broken lines the sharp corners of the hill. The houses on the wall undoubtedly belong to a later date but there have certainly been dwelling houses for daily use there from the very beginning. The tower was also used here as a refuge in case of danger. Its lower storey consists of a lofty arched room accessible through in the apex of the arch. A shaft in the ground might be a well. Such rooms have, as underground prisons, received a romantic glow in fairy tales, ballads and literature. In later times indeed they were used for this very purpose. These dungeons were originally used to store provisions. The great significance of the part played by stores of food and fresh water in a fortress during a long siege was frequently demonstrated in history. The entrance to the tower was on the second storey and was connected with the dwelling houses next to the tower by means of a drawbridge. When danger threatened, people went over into the tower with all their possessions. The drawbridge was then raised and the siege entered into its last and decisive phase. Now it depended on the persistance of the attacks and on the quantity of provisions in the tower as to which side emerged victorious. It very rarely happened that the huge, massive walls of the tower could be breached

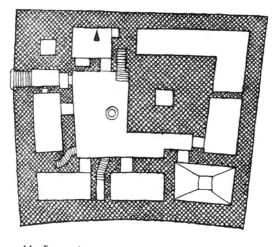

44 · Lower fortress near Rüdesheim, Germany

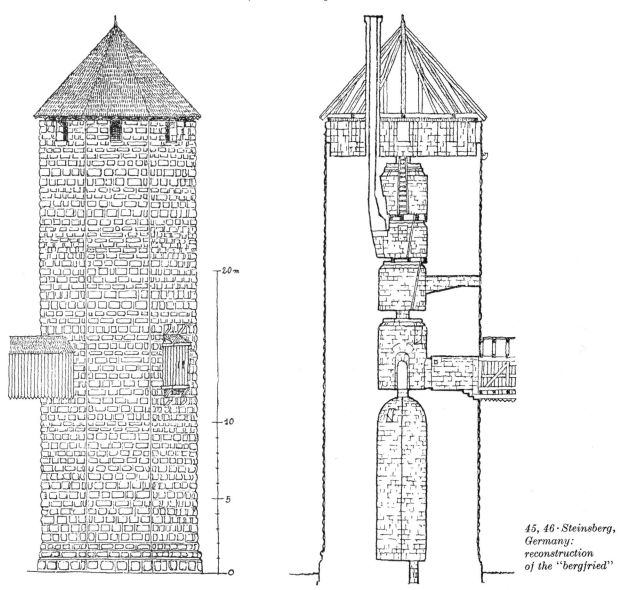

45, 46 · Steinsberg,
Germany:
reconstruction
of the "bergfried"

by mines or siege-engines. Even if the lower part of the tower could be invaded the defenders could still maintain a very effective resistance from the upper storeys. The upper part was only reached through a narrow opening from which the invaders could be attacked with boiling water or pitch, for there was always a chimney in one of the upper storeys. The fighting, however, very rarely reached the inside of the tower; the enemy was usually driven back from the outer walls with stones and boiling water which was hurled from above out of loopholes.

The tower in German-speaking lands was not developed in so majestic a manner as it was in France and England even though it contained rooms for daily use. Several inhabited towers can serve as examples, especially in southern and western districts where this type of tower survived into later periods, for instance Handschuhsheim near Heidelberg, the family towers at Regensburg, Trier, Köln and Mainz. German-speaking Switzerland contributed to this development with a great number of inhabited towers, with the ancestral castle of the imperial Austrian Habsburgs at the top of the list. The simple four-sided tower of Habsburg was built about 1020 and from the very beginning was used as a dwelling place (ill. 178) until a special building was constructed for daily use. The dwelling-tower in the Austrian fortress is in many cases the central point of the lay-out, here also of a simple quality, mostly rectangular in shape; for example Brandis, and Petersberg above Friesach. When it is a question of smaller defence works or observation posts, the tower, in its original form, was always settled upon as the most suitable of all solutions. Towers are to be found, therefore, everywhere from Austria and Switzerland to as far as the Baltic. Church towers were also built for defence. There are two prominent examples in Northern Germany, Marodei in Mecklenburg and Gräfte near Driburg in Westphalia. The first was a typical turreted fortress with a circular moat and a small observation post. Driburg is noteworthy for its regularly planned ramparts and moats, which lend weight to the idea that the fortress was of Roman design. However excavation showed that it was built in the 11th century.

The turreted fortress in Germany was developed parallel with a type of fortress in which the tower played a subordinate part or where it did not exist at all. Citadels without towers are indeed also known in England, where the universal type does not predominate so much, however, as in Germany. The surrounding wall of the shell keeps from the earliest times shows a tendency to grow out of the tower. In Germany, on the other hand, the protection afforded by the surrounding wall takes pride of place throughout the Middle Ages among the elements of fortress defence. In this respect the connection with the *wallburg*, the ancient national fort, is recognizable; the German fortress with the surrounding wall is significantly removed from the Anglo-Norman turreted fortress.

A well-known fortress is Todenmann (ill. 47) laid out at the beginning of the 10th century near Rinteln. The main fortress is almost circular, with an oval advance fort. The former is surrounded by a wall, on the inner side of which a chapel and two rooms cluster for protection. There is also a four-cornered tower here whose main purpose is not defence as it is in corresponding buildings in west German fortresses. A larger tower, on the contrary, stood in the advance fort which was possibly built as a watch tower and *bergfried*. Todenmann's ground plan, therefore, has quite a different appearance from the Anglo-Norman and west German

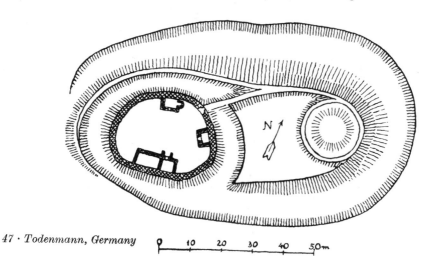

47 · *Todenmann, Germany*   0   10   20   30   40   50m

citadels, where the tower occupied a central position in the fortress. It is tempting to compare this fortress with the fortified Carolingian royal courtyard and their *sala regia* in the middle, behind which is the Roman castle with the *praetorium* in the centre. The Byzantine turreted fortresses also belong to this type. But Todenmann must, according to its construction, trace its descent from the ring-forts of ancient times and indeed from that type called Saxon by Schuchhardt.

Eckartsberga in Thuringia (ill. 48) provides another example of the subordinate role played by the tower. This citadel was also begun in the 10th century. Eckartsberga is situated on

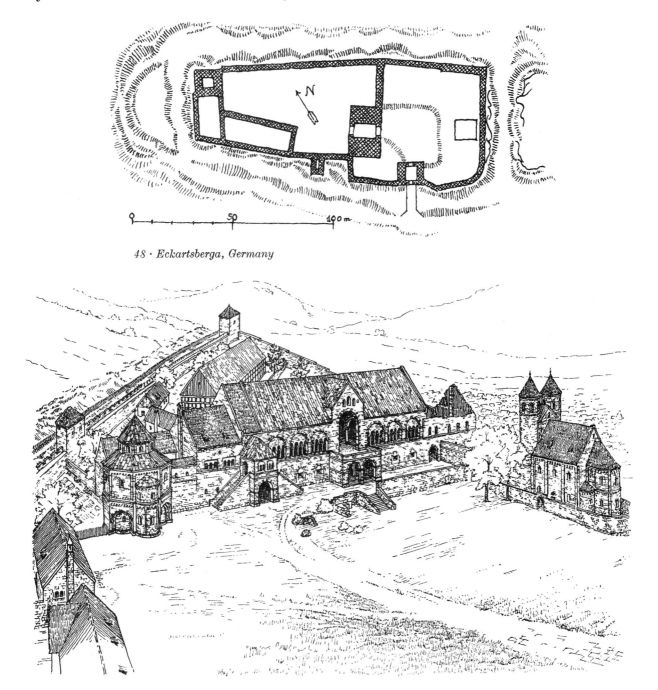

48 · Eckartsberga, Germany

49 · Goslar, Germany: reconstruction of the palace (1230)

an eminence of elliptical shape and, like Todenmann, is arranged in two parts. The lay-out does not follow the contours of the ground. The fortress is an irregular quadrilateral in shape, in which the southern corner of the advance fort is somewhat rounded off. The main tower is sited in the same position as at Todenmann and the watch tower is also in the advance fort, whereas the tower in the main fortress is not markedly conspicuous in proportion to the rest of the building. Especially noteworthy, on the other hand, are the turret-like gateways between the main and advance fortresses.

From the 11th century onwards when the medieval fortress swiftly proceeds to its period of full bloom the protection afforded by tower and surrounding wall is often allied in a way which does not permit a distinction to be made between them. The specifically German citadel is linked with *bergfried*, palace and surrounding wall protection in a number of variations. The connecting links with predecessors on the same spot, the part played by the fortress inside the surrounding settlement and the contours of the ground are the most important factors which give it its shape.

The medieval fortress in its classical form was created through a ceaseless welding together of house and fortress, either in the concentrated form as a turreted fortress or with the help of cordons of walls as the element which linked house and fortress. It was basically the special feature of the military building that it limited the precincts of the fortress to a minimum at the expense of the dwelling houses and outward show. The peaceful Carolingian palace no longer had any justification for an independent existence within the narrow walls of the medieval fortress. The palace probably needed very soon the protection afforded by the surrounding wall, but the two elements are not yet directly connected with one another.

The wall constituted an element in itself and developed into a very large area with independent dwellings. The development of the old palace designs was fashioned in this way after the time of Charlemagne, in particular about 900, when the Norman and Hungarian invasions plagued the country for a decade. But neither the Ottonian nor the Salic period saw any radical transformations from the fortification point of view in comparison with the Carolingian palace designs. Goslar is the most pronounced example of this; in it the magnitude of the imperial power appears in its most highly monumental architectural shape. Goslar, just like Charlemagne's Ingelheim was, in its original form, still unfortified. The main hall, built at the beginning of the 11th century, was probably constructed of wood and then replaced in the reign of Henry III about 1040—1050 by a large stone building. A thorough transformation of the palace took place finally about 1190 owing to dilapidations or a conflagration, and about 1220 the building acquired the great double outside staircases in the court (ill. 49). The present palace contains parts of the wall from these periods and, in spite of the lengthy restoration work of the last century, a good idea of the original appearance of the old palace can be had, owing to Hölscher's researches. The interior of the building consisted of two rooms, the lower of which was used in winter with its small window openings and heating arrangement, while the upper was used as a summer room with its window arcades of imposing size. The last named room was the real *aula regia* and after the reconstruction in the 1190s the transept of the hall was opened up with a curved arcade leading towards a gallery on the side of the courtyard through which the people waiting outside could see into the transept with the imperial throne in the foreground. A living room is connected to the northern gable of the hall and, east of this, a gallery leads to the chapel.

The linking of all these elements is firm and regular, and Goslar is directly connected with the traditions of Charlemagne's time. A new living apartment in the high Romanesque style was added to the southern gable of the hall and it consisted of an assembly room, the Ulrich chapel and a living room proper. Even now the building still retains its essential peaceful character, although both tower and palace of Goslar were surrounded at the beginning of the 12th century by a wall. But this measure had scarcely any influence on the open character of the imperial residence, which never had the appearance of a real fortress.

Henry the Lion about 1175 had the fortress of Dankwarderode built in Brunswick, which, within certain limits, can be considered as a successor to Goslar. The combination of individual principles has, however, now become much more free than in Goslar. One can see in the arrangement of the living rooms, of the houses for men and women, the traditions of the Germanic type of courtyard with special houses for every purpose. Two turreted buildings lend Dankwarderode, more than Goslar, the accentuated appearance of a fortress, which is enhanced by the courtyard with its walls and moats.

For the first time, more than 300 years after the time of Charlemagne, the defence tower was conclusively accorded a place of its own in the palace design and the palace was compressed into the narrow area of the protective wall-cordon so that the peaceful Carolingian royal court and the post-Carolingian knight's fortress were welded together into an imperial fortress, which was both imposing in appearance and capable of defending itself. If, in the early fortresses, defence had been the first consideration, living conditions now had the same importance as defence. There is a classic balance between the two until they later became separated once more. This is at its most balanced even at the time of the Hohenstaufens (1138—1250) and its most illustrious representative is Frederick Barbarossa (died 1190). Charlemagne was for Barbarossa the great model for building activity; architecture should reflect the majesty of the imperial dignity. But times had now changed. The imperial power was no longer so absolute as it had been in the 9th century and the fortresses of the nobility were arrogantly scattered throughout the whole country. The emperor must take part in the race and the imperial citadels began to be erected in a more defiant and invulnerable manner than all the others. Barbarossa started systematically to reconstruct royal fortresses from old ones or else he began to build new fortresses so that a whole chain of strong-points stretched from west to east.

The palaces were now no longer merely political and economic focal points but also cultural. The German knightly way of life was going through its time of greatest splendour. Even the imperial cities which rapidly grew up in the invigorating atmosphere of trade and industry had a share in this upward trend, and every village situated in the vicinity of a palace was raised to the rank of town. Barbarossa created for himself a powerful political focal point on the

Upper Rhine where Haguenau was completed in 1160 as the foremost palace, almost a capital. It seems to be almost of symbolical importance that the ground-plan of this site, now vanished, in Alsace had its prototype in the Aachen of Charlemagne; the building was, like Aachen, polygonal which probably also explains the form of the Hohenstaufen fortress in Sicily, Castel del Monte, to be spoken of later.

Eger is the Hohenstaufen imperial fortress of which we have the best knowledge, thanks to Schürer's researches. The fortress stands on a hill, on which a stone building had already been erected about 1130. Its circular wall was used in the western part of the Hohenstaufen fortress. Eger was elevated to the rank of imperial fortress in the years between 1180 and 1225 as a powerful political base against Bohemia. The ground plan is four-cornered and the strong-point of the defence is situated on the entrance side of the fortress (ill. 59). There the Black Tower (ill. 51) rises up, a kind of *bergfried* with one corner projecting from the curtain wall, which was very popular about 1200. Eger, with its round towers and barbican, was completed in the late Middle Ages. The traditional group of palace, chapel and dwelling house, stands in the courtyard of the fortress, and characteristics of Goslar and Dankwarderode can be recognised once more in its lay-out. But the hall in Eger was not erected solely with regard to outer show for the dwelling house was also, for the first time in the history of palace architecture, united under the same roof, which resulted in the arrangement of the rooms being altered. A characteristic of the Hohenstaufen idea of outward show is that the palace has a wide-open window-arcade fearlessly exposed to the outside, testifying to the love of nature and of views which prevailed at this period. This feature was later often repeated if the landscape was suitable. The chapel belongs undoubtedly to the type of palace already laid down. The interior is divided into an upper and lower chapel which are linked by an opening in the arch. This also reflects the typical medieval way of thinking, which divided people into the distinguished and the less important, into the free nobility and the servants. The union between palace and chapel exists as a symbol of the theocratic outlook with the palace as the representative of political life and the chapel the representative of religious life. The double chapel at Eger may be said to be the finest of its kind. The upper part was first completed under Frederick II and already bears traces of early Gothic characteristics of style. There is also a highly significant chapel of the Hohenstaufen period in the imperial fortress at Nuremburg (ill. 52), where the double chapel and the west gallery of the chapel are united. The lay-out, moreover, is a mixture of different periods with a five-sided tower of cornered stone with bosses on it which belongs to the same period as the Black Tower at Eger.

The building of the imperial palace at Gelnhausen was begun in the 1170s but it took a long time to complete, possibly with several interruptions. Several palace traditions also still survive here, particularly in the union of palace, chapel and dwelling house (ill. 54, 61). Gelnhausen follows the development which had its beginning in Eger. The hall is combined with living rooms which meant that the ground floor had to be provided with an inner gallery. The details in the decoration of the palace can be reckoned as amongst the most significant of the Hohenstaufen period, and show a connection with Alsace and Saxony (Königslutter

50 · Eger, Bohemia: crypt of the fortress

51 · Eger, Bohemia: Black Tower

52 · Nuremburg, Germany: emperor's fortress

53 · Münzenberg, Germany

54 · Gelnhausen, Germany: inside the fortress

*55 · Münzenberg, Germany:
double window in the palace*

56 · Wartburg, Germany: palace

57 · *Vianden, Luxemburg: doorway in the old palace*

58 · *Trifels, Germany*

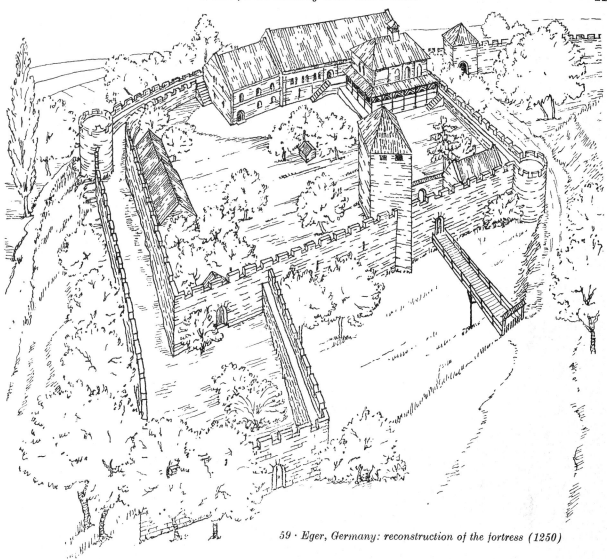

59 · Eger, Germany: reconstruction of the fortress (1250)

school). A delight in detail is everywhere apparent which recalls the earliest wood carvings and is in odd contrast to the huge monumentality of the walls. The chapel is not situated separately in the courtyard but over the entrance arch in the gate-house building. This is a feature which is explained by the medieval idea that God's house will contribute to the defence of the approach. Chapels of this type were often dedicated to St. Michael. A four-cornered tower in the palace group of buildings was the third typical component in the medieval fortress architecture. This tower, as opposed to the chapel, had the duty of protecting the entrance by temporal and not spiritual methods.

A *bergfried* stood in the courtyard of the citadel and it was now accepted as a natural feature even in the imperial palace. The surrounding wall of the citadel near the *bergfried* is so situated that the outer defence cordon could be protected from the tower.

Münzenberg, Büdingen, Trifels, Wildenberg, Wimpfen and several other imperial fortresses of the Hohenstaufen are also fine examples of this period with its brilliantly successful

combination of defence, love of artistic decoration and size (ill. 53, 55, 62, 63). The palace everywhere occupies a dominating position with its wide open arcades giving a long view and its
walls frequently built of squared stone with bosses. The palace at Wildenberg can be reckoned
among the finest creations of its time but Trifels also ranks among the best and most ample
lay-outs (ill. 58, 60).

Trifels is one of the famous 'Trinity of Fortresses'. Trifels, Anebos and Scharfenberg are
all situated on rocky heights and undoubtedly on the remains of older fortresses. Even if
the lie of the land did not permit any freer grouping together of palace, chapel and residence,
all these three different buildings were here compressed in the confined area of the fortress.
The great distinctive staircase, which was usually in front of the palace building, here leads
up to the tower, the lower storey of which contains the entrance to the palace. Over this
was the imperial chapel with a finely shaped apse on the outer side of the tower. The imposing
ruined citadel of Vianden (Luxemburg) also illustrates the artistic achievements of the

60 · Trifels, Germany: reconstruction

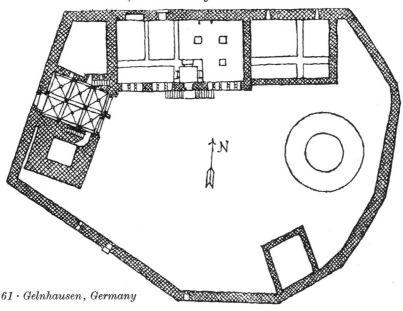

61 · *Gelnhausen, Germany*

Hohenstaufen period which is seen particularly in the early 13th century portal in the older palace (ill. 57).

As for the ground plan, in this respect there is no definitely prominent Hohenstaufen type. The natural advantages are readily made use of for defensive purposes and the surrounding wall and the protective tower conform, to a certain extent, to the shape of the plateau.

Nature, however, is not followed too closely; the ideal shape is oval, polygonal or four-cornered, even when these shapes are not executed with mathematical exactitude. If the plateau is inclined to be long this may well lead to the building of two *bergfrieds* as at Münzenberg, which was built 1160 (ill. 62). Moreover, preference is given to the polygonal shape with the palace and the *bergfried* as the centre, as at Gelnhausen. Wildenberg, built after 1168, achieved the classic purity of the castle type (ill. 63), which in this case can be considered an exception, for the German citadel showed itself from the very beginning as easily adaptable to the contours of the ground: the *bergfried*, with its emphasis on defence from a height, best fulfils its role when it occupies the highest possible position. The surrounding wall was, for its part, not limited to any straight lines, for there were no flanking towers which alone would have demanded a free view from tower to tower along the line of the wall. These technical details, however, do not fully explain the development of the ground plan of the German fortress. Defensive considerations were not always the only reasons which caused German citadels to be built in the mountains where, to a certain extent, they formed part of the natural scenery. Unknown forces were behind this, forces which elsewhere helped to bring the mighty Norman donjon and the cube-shaped conciseness of form south of the Alps. The combination of military purposes and those of outward show was demonstrated clearly by the Wartburg, the main residence of the Landgraf of Thüringen. This fortress, with its rich historical associations and, in spite of its unsuccessful restoration, its still imposing buildings, is one of the best known German fortresses of the Middle Ages (ill. 56, 64). Nature, here, has also played a part in influencing the form of the ground

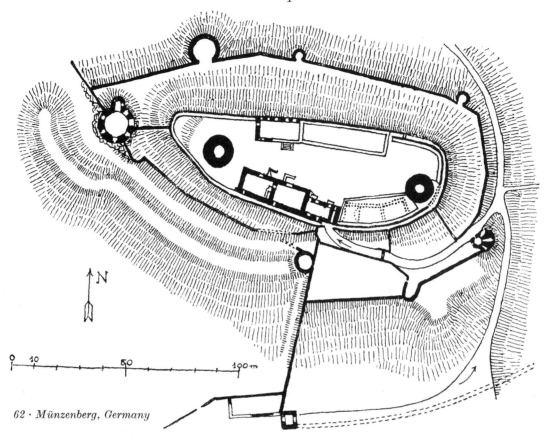

62 · Münzenberg, Germany

plan by means of a rather long, steep mountain height. The Wartburg was started in the 11th century and its most important building, the Landgraf's house, dates from the time of Landgraf Hermann I (1190—1217); it forms an important link in the chain of palaces which developed historically from the palace of Goslar through those of Eger and Gelnhausen. It rises up on the eastern side where the vertical rock-face is perfectly adapted to defence and makes a surrounding wall superfluous. The great windows of the palace open arrogantly on the exterior façade, while the courtyard side has three rows of similarly curved arcades. The palace was built in this form as much for living in as for external show, which led to minor galleries being constructed on the courtyard side, not only in the lower part as at Gelnhausen but on all three storeys. The window arcades on the courtyard side consequently did not open directly into the halls but had loggias between—a feature firmly established in the south but hardly suited to the northern climate. The upper banqueting hall was undoubtedly only used in summer which may also have been the case with the famous Hall of the Singers in the middle storey. There were rooms suitable for everyday use on the ground floor, and the women's quarters (*camera caminata*) were heated by a fireplace. The Wartburg was, until 1406, the permanent residence of the prince. Later high officials and military commanders lived there. Generation after generation has left behind its own ornamentation in the courtyards of the fortress and a good idea can be obtained from this mosaic how knightly grandeur was gradually replaced by bourgeois standards of living; in the small rooms it was entirely superseded by the late medieval townsman's way of living.

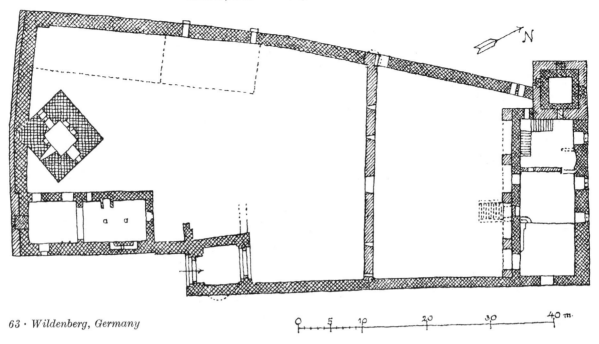

63 · *Wildenberg, Germany*

The stone-built fortress began to be constructed also in Scandinavia about the middle of the 12th century. A feudal system after the central and western European pattern did not, however, develop and building was carried out more by the political and ecclesiastical authorities. The new citadels must frequently be considered as direct successors to the earlier northern national fortresses which, in many cases, were still used throughout the whole period of the Middle Ages. Various types occur, such as the circular fortress, entrenchments on rocky heights and also motte lay-outs, the latter especially in Denmark. Among the prehistoric designs in Denmark there is a highly original fortress at Trelleborg, with a circular ground plan of regular design, inside whose walls traces of foundations have

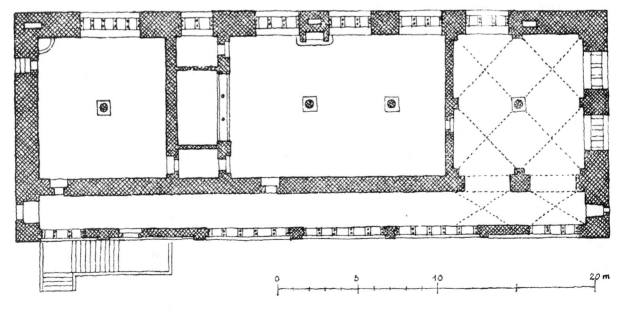

64 · *Wartburg, Germany: palace*

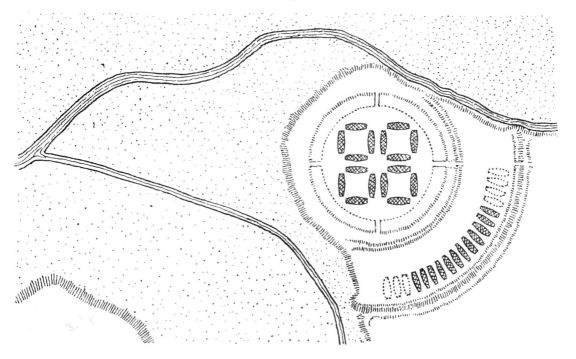

65 · Trelleborg, Denmark: Viking fortress

been found which are divided up into regular squares (ill. 65). The inspiration probably
came from Roman lay-outs in England where the Danish Vikings often established their
camps on old Roman camp sites. Trelleborg can therefore be considered as a characteristic
hybrid between ring-fort and castle.

Söborg in Zeeland (ill. 66) is one of the oldest of Danish stone-built fortresses. It was founded
about the middle of the 12th century by Archbishop Eskil in Lund. Only an octagonal
tower previously stood on the spot, built on a foundation of two four-cornered frames made
of oak beams. In Eskil's time this strong point grew into a large establishment, with a
surrounding wall in the form of a broken quadrilateral and a palace in front of the east side
of the wall with a staircase in the middle; on the north side there was a round building,
probably a chapel. A smaller house, divided into two, lay to the south of the palace and this
house was for everyday use. The whole bears a striking resemblance to the palace in Goslar
which Eskil undoubtedly used as a model. Söborg was further enlarged about 1200.

Of the remaining Danish lay-outs of the 12th century, the oldest fortress in Copenhagen
was circular including a hill within the surrounding wall in the style of the motte lay-out.
There is a similar design in Vordingborg. Lilleborg at Bornholm more than any other
recalls the Saxon fortresses; it originated in the second half of the 12th century and was
almost destroyed in 1259.

There had been connections at an early date with the countries of the classic turreted fortress
in the west, but North Germany also provided a certain amount of inspiration. Several of the
Danish *voldsteder* were of motte design in the 12th century, often with a wooden tower as the
main building. Motte fortresses are also to be found in southern Sweden, for instance at

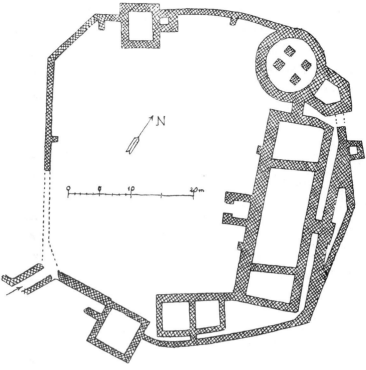

66 · Söborg, Denmark

Sölvesborg. But stone-built turreted fortresses were already being built at quite an early date. The earliest and most noteworthy tower of this type in Denmark was at Bastrup in North Zeeland, of which only the lower part has survived. The tower was probably built at the time of Waldemar I (1157—1182) which was recognised as a time of universal progress in military building. Waldemar built several turreted fortresses, for example, Sprogö and Taarnborg, to protect important districts and waterways. It was in his reign that the art of brick building in Denmark was established and the long frontier wall known as Waldemar's Wall at Danne- werk, near Schleswig, is renowned as the king's most famous work. It was Waldemar also who was revered as the mighty conqueror of the Slavs. The dramatic final struggle for the chief lair of the Wendish pirates on Rügen Island, the sacred citadel of Arkona, is described by the chronicler Saxo Grammaticus.

The turreted fortress in Sweden underwent great and important development under Knut Eriksson towards the end of the 12th century. Fortresses were now established at a series of strategic points along the east coast of Sweden to protect the country from the attacks of the heathen pirates from Kurland and Ösel. These turreted fortresses are renowned for their foundation walls as are those at Stockholm, Kalmar and Borgholm, where they were succeeded by large fortresses. A quantity of smaller, rounder or rectangular towers were erected on the island of Gotland which must have played a part as refuge towers, storehouses and light-houses. They were named *kastals*, which proves their connection with the development on the mainland of Europe, but they cannot have been built earlier than about 1200.

A start was made at the end of the 12th century on the erection of composite lay-outs of the castle type. Nyborg in Denmark is a citadel of this kind. It was rebuilt in the 16th century, but its foundation walls, with the turret-shaped half towers and a gatehouse tower on the eastern side, must have originated in the late romanesque period. A palace was built against the west walls. Significant remains of a late romanesque palace have been found in Drags-holm, which also had a surrounded wall.

THE GOTHIC FORTRESS
CRUSADER CASTLES

In their advance on the Holy Land from 1096 to 1099 the European knights came into close contact for the first time with the eastern art of fortification. New problems of defence arose as the vast armies streamed in from all parts of Western Europe. An exchange of ideas was bound to follow. For a long time, therefore, the importance of the Crusades as an influence on western castle design has been much debated. The truth probably lies between the two extremes of over- and under-estimation. The contact between west and east was never entirely broken in the Middle Ages, particularly in the earlier period, when great parts of the West, together with their culture, lay under the oppressive weight of the East from which they could only free themselves slowly and with difficulty. The crusades renewed the contact with the East, although in a different manner.

The old traditions of late antiquity had survived through Byzantium in the east and had been further developed by Arab architects. Several cities were protected by huge city walls which had been planned according to a well-tried Roman pattern. Many city walls built by the Romans in Europe had been well preserved but the progressive development had up till then not yet included the principles of defence which were therein demonstrated. Constantinople must have made a deep impression on the crusaders for everything that the East had to offer in the way of defence architecture was concentrated in the so-called 'landwall' (ill. 67, 73). This stepped wall was built in the reign of Emperor Theodosius II about 412 and was later restored after being damaged in an earthquake. The steeply rising protective

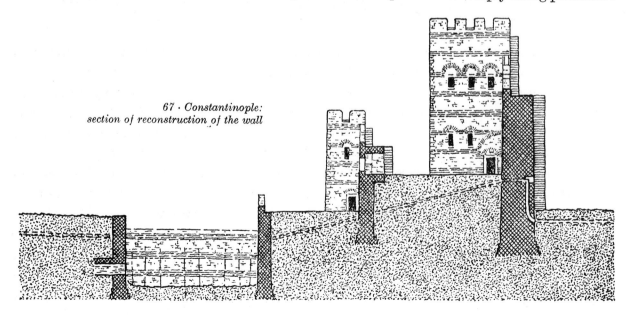

67 · Constantinople:
section of reconstruction of the wall

*68 · Antioch,
Syria: town wall*

cordon is still extant and consists of a main wall with projecting towers and a great deal
of wall and moat protection in front of it. The barbican is here seen in a clearly defined form
and this ancient eastern element was later incorporated into western fortress architecture
by the crusaders. It cannot be claimed, however, that the barbican before this period was
entirely unknown in Northern Europe—it was already present in the citadels of antiquity,
but it was missing once more in the early medieval turreted and walled fortresses.

In 1097 the crusaders fought in front of the walls of Nicaea and Antioch (ill. 68) which were of
Byzantine and had projecting wall turrets close together with straight sections
of the wall between them. In contrast with the north European free flowing wall-line the use
of the flanking tower principle here results in straight wall sections, with the wall towers
as the co-ordinating defence points. Amongst other details of military building which
the crusaders encountered for the first time were machicolations, or defence galleries projecting from the wall, which were provided with a series of loop-holes—this was also a newly

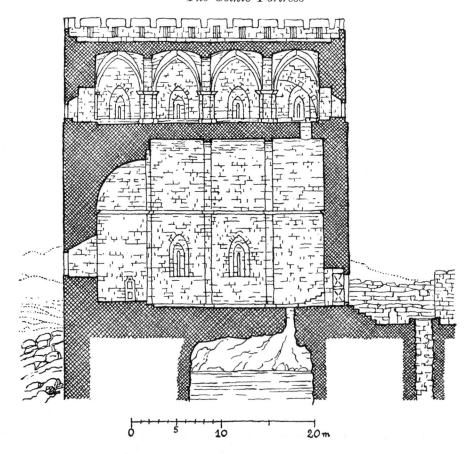

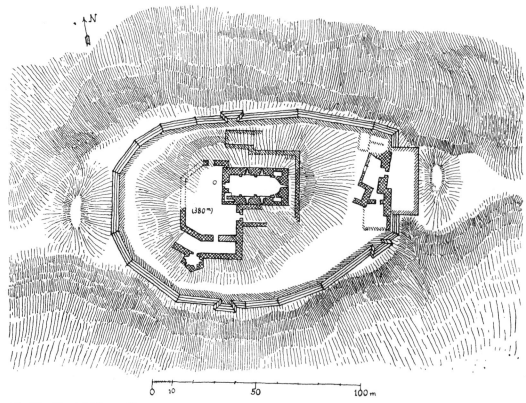

69, 70 · Chastel Blanc, Syria

acquired detail which was later to figure outstandingly in western fortress architecture. The new lessons were not immediately put into practice. People had become so wedded to the old native traditions of building that it was not so easy for them to adapt themselves to all the new things which they ecountered. At first they adopted what was most closely related to their own ideas, so that they only gradually assimilated the new methods. Thus it happened that fortresses were built, as it were, on the border-line between two great periods both of which contributed to the form they took. The fortresses in the Holy Land began to take shape according to the tasks of the various knightly orders. First among these orders, the Order of St. John, was dedicated to a labour of love and charity. Its members, however, after they had carried out these tasks, armed themselves for the protection of pilgrims. The French order of the Templars was founded in 1119 and the Teutonic Order at the end of the 12th century. The Teutonic Order had taken over its precepts mainly from the Templars. But a fully developed feudal system was also brought to Syria, Palestine and Greece which was carried out with very far-reaching consequences. Colonies of French noblemen evolved from the crusader kingdoms.

The fact that France was a leading participant in the crusades can also be seen in architecture. The old Norman keep is prominent among the fortresses introduced by the crusaders, although somewhat altered by local circumstances. Chastel Blanc (Safita) built at the end of the 12th century consists of a huge main tower on a mountain top surrounded by an enclosing wall which follows the contour of the mountain (ill. 69, 70). The wall has no flanking towers. The old central-plan system of defence is still adhered to. The keep was at the same time both chapel and defence point recalling in its shape the fortified churches of Southern France. Among other well-known turreted fortresses in the Holy Land, Tortosa (12th century) Blanche Garde, Sagetta and Giblet were prominent. The last-named has flanking corner towers in which older building remains were partly employed. In several other cases the old Roman-Arab frontier castle was the pattern.

The Crusader fortresses soon became larger than their predecessors. There was a rigid system of organisation in which economic and labour problems were easily solved, which was not the case at home. It soon appeared that in the long run a turreted fortress or a small desert castle was not enough; more space was needed for the soldiers and for the local population. These castles also made a great contribution to the development of trade. Now the large and complex fortress lay-out was created, often situated on a lofty mountain with a fusion in its composition of old and new defence elements.

Considerable remains of these fortresses are still in preservation, of which the most important have been the subject of profound research by Paul Deschamps.

The best known is Krak des Chevaliers (Kalat el Hosn) in northern Syria (ill. 71, 75, 76). This fortress of the knights of St. John has several times been severely damaged by earthquakes and it is principally these natural catastrophes which gave the various periods of building their external appearance. The oldest part of the fortress is to be found in the middle section, the ground plan of which forms a triangle with rounded corners. This part was built in the second half of the 12th century (before 1170). There were four-cornered

71 · Krak des Chevaliers, Syria: reconstruction

buildings on the wall, and the fortress chapel was situated in one of these buildings on the eastern side. The whole of the inside of the wall had small houses in it and there was a hall on the west side of the court which in the first period of its building was not yet complete. Krak des Chevaliers appeared in its completed form at the beginning of the 13th century. On the southern side of the middle section two massive keep-like towers with semi-circular exteriors were added. In order to avoid damage from future earthquakes this most important part of the fortress was situated on an enormous wall foundation with a sloping exterior. A belt of wall with semi-circular flanking towers was built round the older part, which formed a clearly defined barbican of a new model. On the entrance side, towards the east, old buildings have partly influenced the new lay-out in which the flank-protecting principle has consequently not been carried out. The gateway topped by a round tower which was so typical of later periods is also lacking and the machicolations do not yet form any continuous frieze. On the other hand, the west front, with its semi-circular towers, already bears the clearly marked style of the 13th century as it was later encountered everywhere in France. The architecture in the interior is entirely French; this is most obvious in the great hall and its gallery which can be compared most easily with Cistercian architecture with its groined arches of delicate outline and well constructed window openings (ill. 75). French naturalism shows in the very pure style of the capitals. All the details of the fortress were not completed under the Knights of St. John but the Arabs subsequently finished various small points in the outer wall belt.

A succession of other composite fortresses somewhat similar to Krak des Chevaliers was built, suitable for the new elements of defence. Château de Margat (Markab) is very similar to Krak des Chevaliers, in the details of its fortification; both buildings were begun at almost the same time. The keep was also incorporated here in the front of the fortress to face any invaders. The chapel and other buildings are grouped around the courtyard, which in its shape resembles Krak des Chevaliers. On the north side a small tower is connected to the fortress and its surrounding wall with semi-circular flanking towers obviously dates from the beginning of the 13th century.

The fortress of Montfort (Starkenberg) of the Teutonic Order was established in 1229 by the Master of the Order, Hermann von Salza who in 1228 followed the Hohenstaufen monarch Frederick II to the Holy Land (ill. 72). Montfort has often been described as a Rhineland fortress transplanted to Syria, which to a certain extent is true, but must however be accepted with certain reservations. In Montfort also new features already came into their own, principally the surrounding wall. Here, instead of soft European lines as was the case with most of the citadels described above, we have to deal with a turreted

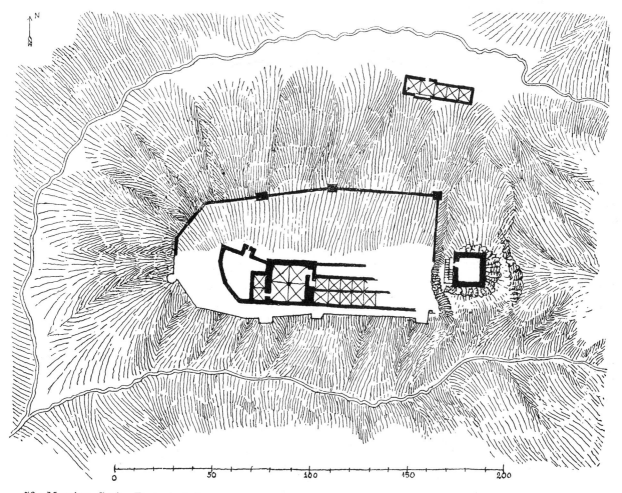

72 · *Montfort, Syria: Teutonic fortress*

wall in straight stretches. In the isolated watch tower, however, outside the main fortress we came across a pure north European feature, a watch tower of the same type as that at Todenmann. The interior of the fortress has not yet been thoroughly examined. To judge from the ground plan the main building consisted of a dwelling tower with an arched chamber on the ground floor, a room which, with its cruciform arches supported by a central pillar, is an example of a lay-out later to be repeated time and time again in the fortresses of the German knightly orders.

The crusaders' building activity reaches its peak at the end of the 12th century and beginning of the 13th. If an enumeration were made of their huge fortress lay-outs, city walls, camps and smaller defence works, a very long list would result, a fact which must have indisputably influenced the universal progress of military building in the west.

As has already been pointed out earlier the combination of wall and tower as regards the flanking principle is a new feature just as much as the barbican and the machicolations. The power of resistance of the fortress was raised to a high level by the introduction of these new elements, which had been introduced in turn to counter new fighting methods and an improvement in weapons, for example, the crossbow. Many things point to the fact that the further development of the castle in the west received an undoubted stimulus from the renewed contact with old Roman-Byzantine traditions. All this, however, would probably not have led on its own to such basic revaluations in Europe if other factors had not come into play, to break up what had been added by the Romanesque style and to make a beginning with the slender, delicate constructions of the Gothic period, as can be seen in the fortress wall and tower.

The planners in Venice had headed the Fourth Crusade towards Greece where, after the foundation of a Latin empire in Constantinople in 1204, the Frankish conquerors had introduced a feudal system which already bore traces of degeneration. As Andrews' researches have shown, the Peloponnese, the medieval district of Morea, contains in its mighty fortress lay-outs frequent examples from the development from Hellenism through Byzantium up to the new creations of the Normans. The centre of the citadel often consists of a massive tower of the keep type, a style of building which was widely distributed by the erection of a chain of Frankish family citadels. On the Acrocorinthus the large heap of ruins is still dominated by a dwelling tower of this type which was built by William Villehardouin (ill. 74). Several other fortresses, Kalamata and Mistra which remained in the hands of Byzantium, also possess relics of similar four-cornered towers. The enlarged polygonal keep of Chlemoutsi (Clermont), with its great barrel-vault encompassing the whole edifice, was built about 1220—23 and is distinguished by the same colonial-cistercian style of building which was quite at home in the Holy Land (Krak des Chevaliers). The fortress of Dótia on the island of Chios in the Aegean Sea, the private property of the Latin emperor Balduin of Flanders in 1204, serves as a typical example of how the keep gained a firm footing also in other parts of 'Nova Francia' (ill. 86). A tower for living purposes stands in the middle of the square, similar to that of Adernò in Sicily. The walls of this tower rest

73 · *Constantinople: Theodosian wall*

74 · *Acrocorinthus, Greece*

75 · *Krak des Chevaliers, Syria:*
gallery outside the Great Hall

76 · *Krak des Chevaliers, Syria*

77 · *Assisi, Italy: Rocca Maggiore*

78 · *Lucera, Italy: surrounding wall*

79 · *Torre Astura, Italy*

80 · Termoli, Italy: tower fortress

81 · Castel del Monte, Italy

82 · *Castel del Monte, Italy: doorway of the Great Hall*

83 · *Catania, Sicily: Hall of Castel Ursino*

84 · Catania, Sicily: Castel Ursino

85 · Fontanellato, Italy

on a pyramid-shaped plinth, an architectural feature which was introduced quite early in Mediterranean countries, so as to prevent damage by earthquake. The lower storey is divided into two longish barrel-vaults and there is an arched-over hall with two aisles. As at Chlemoutsi there is a chimney, which reveals a knowledge of northern customs. This can be noticed also in the dwelling towers in Sicily. The surrounding wall is probably somewhat later than the tower and was built before 1225 when the Byzantines from Nicaea overran the island. The citadels of the other great vassal territories have not yet been explored.

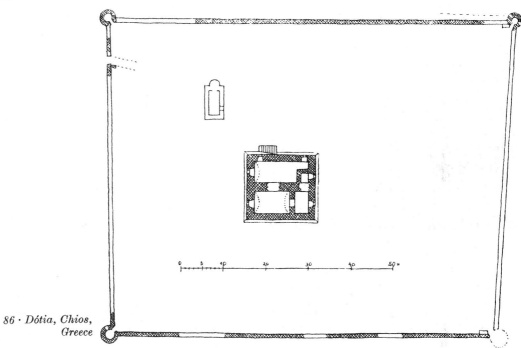

86 · *Dótia, Chios, Greece*

ITALY

The utilisation of natural conditions, as a principle, is not as apparent in Italy as in the Germanic countries. A standard type of construction is found on mountain tops, but only in exceptional cases are found the picturesque attractive groups which prevail in Germany, and even these are not necessarily occasioned by the regional conditions. A few early North Italian fortresses are closely related in their type to the fortress architecture north of the Alps. German style has probably influenced the fortress of Caminate, with its turret like a watch tower and comfortable main buildings. The fortress is mentioned for the first time in documents of the year 1213. The fortresses in Montecuccoli, Montalto-Dora and Velate also show German stylistic peculiarities. Soave, in the province of Verona, is German in its basic design, possessing a watch tower and main building, but still without wall turrets and with greater rectilinearity throughout than is general in Germany. Amongst other fortresses found in the region, one may mention San Leo and Canossa, in the province of Reggio-Emilia, both of very early design. In Canossa, the tendency to regularity of construction should not be dismissed; in the outer surrounding wall one finds flanked towers of Syrian design (ill. 87). Mussomeli in Sicily, which lies like an eagle's nest on top of a steep cliff, may be mentioned as a typical example; but even here attention has been paid to a certain regularity in design. The houses form a hexagon with a donjon on the watch tower. Rocca Maggiore, at Assisi, (ill. 77) where Frederick II lived as guest and hostage of Conrad von Leutsen from 1197 to 1198, is a completely symmetrical fortress. The exterior of Rocca Maggiore shows an insensitive massiveness which has grown from an active striving for power, as in most of the feudal fortresses of the Middle Ages, which were built with the utmost human endeavour. The isolated silhouette is sharply drawn against the sky, horizontally emphasised. If one makes a comparison with the designs in the Palatine countries, the main features are designs based on southern pine or the north European firtrees.

The towered fortress, although not perfected in the same way as the turrets in Normandy and in England, plays a significant part throughout the whole of the Middle Ages in Italy. There, even in the late Middle Ages, the turrets retain their military character, and only occasionally is the building adapted for living purposes. With defence in mind, the turrets retain their design from the beginning of the Middle Ages or even earlier.

In the Roman countryside *turri saracineschi* were found modified slightly to be used as baronial quarters. Amongst the constructions of the late Middle Ages there are such famous examples as Ninfa, built in the 13th century, in the town known as the Pompeii of the time. The keep is surrounded by a wall built in a rectangle and represents a fortress design which already existed in Byzantium in the 6th century. Torre Astura, one of the most romantic fortresses of Italy, originates in an old design (ill. 79). The fortress was probably founded as a protection against Mohammedan sea pirates, and served later as a sea fortress against the Turks. Even up to the end of the Middle Ages there were turret fortresses on all the coasts of Italy; fortresses were often converted out of lighthouses, for example in Genoa, and bridges which were important from a military aspect were built with towers. The tower retains its hold on provincial fortresses, partly following the German watch tower and partly as a forerunner of the residential tower. Thus, for example, in the castle of Montecchio Vesponi, in the province of Arezzo, such a tower is situated next to

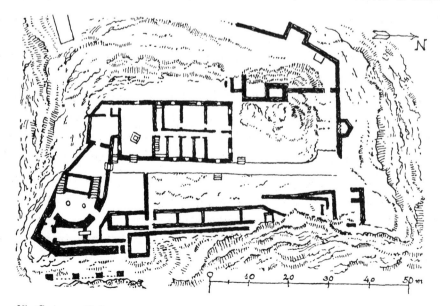

87 · Canossa, Italy

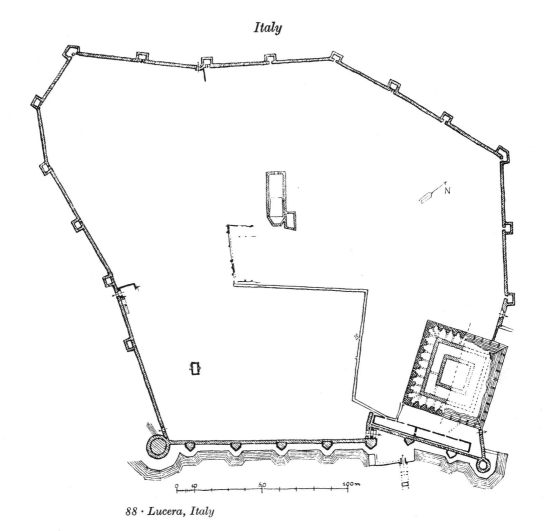

88 · Lucera, Italy

the main building. Its thin shape and the drawbridge to the main building are a further proof of the pastoral origin of the family tower.

Even Frederick II actively followed the tower tradition in his constructions. Nevertheless, it may be seen that his endeavours are not a mere mechanical repetition of existing designs. His era is unusually creative in military building, and in the development of turret fortresses. The young monarch, interested in art, maintained a close relationship with France and England. However, although it was known that he had close connections with France, he had also inherited many of the trends of the Sicilian Normans. It is known that he had Benedictine converts from France in his service , but it is also known that he used to appear like a Calif with verses from the Koran embroidered on his vivid Oriental gown. In the crusade of 1228—29 he had an excellent opportunity to study the tremendous new constructions in Syria, which however did nothing to diminish his great admiration for the fortress constructions of the Arabs. His ties with the Holy Land were even more strengthened in 1229 by his coronation as King of Jerusalem.

In view of these facts we are able to get a better insight into the fortress architecture of Frederick II in Southern Italy. As an example of the further development of a tower stronghold one must first mention Lucera, which was founded in 1235 and later enlarged

89 · Termoli, Italy   0   5   10   15 *m*

under Charles of Anjou (ill. 78, 88). The actual castle, which consists of a tremendous tower, originated from Hohenstaufen days and only the foundation wall remains. It is due entirely to the investigations of Haseloff that we have a fairly clear picture of the castle Lucera as it was at the time of Frederick II. The square tower with a central courtyard rests on a very high massive base, shaped rather like a pyramid. The basic design reminds us of the Normans' enlarged strongholds, and we have every reason to suppose that Frederick II was influenced here by the Syrian example. Strictly speaking, therefore, Lucera is not a turreted fort, but something between a tower and a square-fort. It was planned not only as a fortress but as a residence for the Emperor, and contained beautiful rich Gothic arches throughout a number of regularly placed rooms. The tower fortress of Termoli was also designed by Frederick II, about 1247 (ill. 80, 89). Just as in Lucera, the tower here also rests on a high pyramid-shaped base which in itself forms a fortification building with large casemates and a water cistern in the centre. Termoli, however, does not possess an inner courtyard as in Lucera, and there are also differences in many other respects. After an earthquake in 1456, Termoli was reconstructed, and according to Haseloff has not been accurately restored. The tower shape of Lucera and Termoli has been copied in many places in Southern Italy, as for instance in Tertiveri, Castelfiorentino and Montecorvino. Further examples are either incorporated in later fortresses or lie in ruins.

With the emphasis very much on a military character the strongholds in southern Italy attained new shape under Frederick II in 1230. Owing to a centralised system of administration, a great number of imperial fortresses rose for the officials and militia of the ruler. All construction of private fortresses was forbidden, which partly contributed to a one-sided execution of design directed by the central administration. Amongst these Hohenstaufen castles, there were a number of coastal and military bases, foremost that at Bari which is particularly worth mentioning. It was constructed in 1233, and consists of a castle with rectangular corner turrets and a courtyard surrounded by buildings (ill. 90). This castle represents a type which was later to be the leading design in the whole of Italy. Its relationship to the Roman-Arab castles in Syria, for example Kasr-Bcher, is not to be overlooked, and besides the basic design there are also details which give evidence of the decorative Arabic influence. At the same time as Bari, fortresses were constructed in Trani and Brindisi. In all these fortresses, the emphasis is so clearly on defence that they have been used partly for military purposes up to the present day, and this has often resulted in additional building and alteration. A further example of the same style is to be found in Gioia del Colle which was completed after 1230.

The fortress at Catania occupies a special place among the four winged Hohenstaufen fortresses, known to be constructed in 1239 (ill. 83, 84, 91). It is also known that the Emperor demanded from his masterbuilder Lentini that the fortress should be 'comfortably' built, meaning that it should be adapted for domestic more than for purely military purposes. This is indeed the case, for the interior of the fortress at Catania includes large halls in which the French Gothic influence has created a strongly uniform interior. The basic design is mathematically precise: the hall forms a square, and the whole lay-out is systematic apart from the arch details. The defence is conducted from symmetrically situated turrets. There are four large round towers, one at each corner, and a like number of small semi-circular turrets in the middle of the outer walls. Here basic design has achieved a consequent symmetry which may be compared with Roman designs, making contact with an antique heritage, probably through the medium of the East (Djebel-Seis, ill. 12). However, the French vault construction has welded the old elements into a new unit, with the clean spans of the Gothic system much used in ecclesiastical buildings. The castle at Syracuse confirms that Frederick II built under a great many influences. The surrounding wall here also forms a square with four strong round towers at the corners, and there is no courtyard. The interior consists of one huge hall divided by twenty-five square vaulted arches which are supported by massive round pillars. Although there are no examples of such architecture to be found in France, there are many in the Orient, in the pillared halls of the mosques (ill. 92).

Of all the fortresses created by Frederick II, his most personal is the famous Castel del Monte, built in 1240 as a hunting castle on a steep mountain in Apulia (ill. 81, 82, 93). The Castel del Monte is symmetrical and clearly silhouetted against the sky, and is regarded by all art historians as a symbol of the Hohenstaufen reign in Southern Italy. The basic design is octagonal, with uniformly shaped towers on each corner, and surrounding walls which are parallel with the inner lines of the building. The arrangement of the rooms is as symmetrical as the surrounding walls. Castel del Monte distinguishes itself by the same constant regularity as the fortress at Catania, only here it appears as a central building. The basic design has often been called theoretical, and many have supposed that it was the Emperor himself who drew the plans for this, his favourite castle, but this is a supposition which has never really been confirmed. It has, however, never been disputed that on frequent occasions the Emperor himself gave direct instructions to his masterbuilders. Many features of Castel del Monte are French, for instance the interior architecture, where we can recognise the Benedictine influence both in the extraordinary stylistically exact arches and in other artistically executed details (ill. 82). The strongly emphasised residential character must also be pointed out. The basic plan betrays a certain affinity to the castle at Boulogne, built in 1231, although this has not the mathematically clear arrangement of Castel

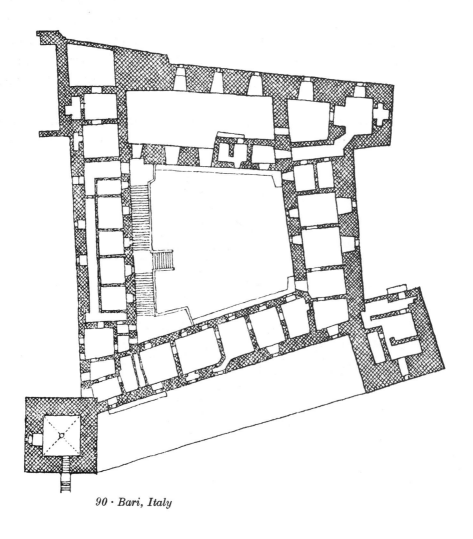

90 · Bari, Italy

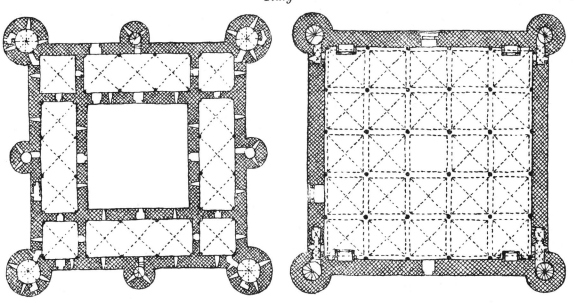

91 · Catania, Sicily: Castel Ursino   *92 · Syracuse, Sicily: fortress*

del Monte, where the spacing of the vaults led to a certain reservation of basic design which is comparable to that of a Gothic cathedral. The Hohenstaufen's favourite palace in the Palatinate, Haguenau, may have influenced the basic design, but the idea of the enlarged tower stronghold was already in existence at Lucera, and could up to a certain point be compared with the development of the shell keep in England. The result however, became an independent new creation which could be compared to neither the one nor the other prototype.

Charles I of Anjou, 1226—1285, partly extended Hohenstaufen building. Amongst others, the citadel at Lucera was erected by him, and consists of a strong surrounding wall complete

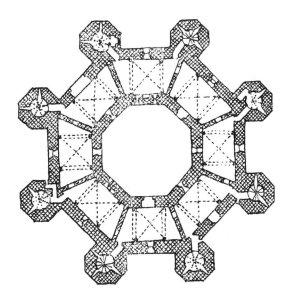

93 · Castel del Monte, Italy

94. Arques,
France: reconstruction

with turrets which derived from a Hohenstaufen castle (ill. 78). The wall was erected between 1269 and 1275 under the leadership of the French masterbuilder Pierre d'Angicourt, whose origin explains the French formation of the wall turrets, although the vertical defence was not extended as much as in those built at the same time in France. From smaller reconstructions of other Hohenstaufen fortresses, we know that the French examples now became even more popular in southern Italy.

The four-winged stronghold with corner turrets appeared in northern and central Italy rather later than in Sicily. In the first place, there were the town castles, and side by side with the purely military fortresses a new type arose, namely a palace with a court surrounded by a loggia. The influence was partly that of the building tradition of Frederick II, and partly the direct contact with the many variations of Byzantine style. In the 13th century, it was usual for the dwellings of the nobility to consist of a palace building connected to a turret (*palatium cum turri*) that is to say a type in which the old isolated towers have been connected to a palace. From the end of the 13th century onwards, the palace was changed to a building with a central courtyard and frequently with corner turrets. In the 14th century, just as in France, the defence passage with loopholes resting on corbels became general, and in conjunction with the typically Italian 'swallowtail' pinnacles give a vivid cadence to the crowning of the massive walls. A marked similarity in the composition usually distinguishes such castles, among which we find the castle of Ferrara, 1383, with its rectangular corner towers and, in a freer way, Fontanellato (ill. 85). The castles of Ivrea and Piedmont (Castello di Montalto Dora) present a more threatening and war-like front. Their round, slender corner towers can be traced back to French examples. The towns, too, saw themselves forced by internal strife to extend the public communal buildings into fortresses. The famous Palazzo Vecchio in Florence (started in 1298, but frequently added to and altered later) is one of the first examples in this category.

FRANCE

About 1200, France's building style in fortresses takes a new turn which is inspired by the same vital intensity as ecclesiastical building. The new style drew its inspiration partly from the Holy Land. Either the existing forms of building were abandoned or a blend of old and new was created. The endeavours of the Gothic style to create more comfortable living conditions find strongest expression in France, where the residential purpose is given increasing precedence by the flourishing fortunes of the Knights and a heightened feeling for nature. The place of the old donjon is taken by a compound structure where, for a time, military and residential parts are of equal importance, until there gradually comes a division which results in the building on the one hand of open castles and on the other of purely military fortresses.

The flanking tower had the same basic significance for the new development in fortress architecture as the pointed arch in church building. A mere glance at the fortresses of the Holy Land shows how the whole defence system is dominated by flanking towers which hold the basic design together. A direct result of this was the rebirth of the rectangular type, though not always as an unavoidable condition. For various reasons the flanking tower could be united with other basic designs, but a straight wall nearly always stretched from tower to tower. Already at the beginning of the 13th century, under the severe reign of Philippe Auguste (1180—1223), the new system was seriously taken up and found suited to the Capetians in their determined endeavours to maintain national unity in the face of feudal dissolution. Gaillard was one of the first French fortresses whose defence structures were strengthened by round towers (ill. 20). Among the other donjons which were extended according to the new principles one must name Arques which was also completed in the first half of the 13th century (ill. 94). The old Romanesque donjon of about 1125 remained standing as the main building. The new parts were intended primarily to provide rooms for the enlarged domestic economy. The increased demand for princely and representative dwellings was therefore not fulfilled; the fortress continues to be first and foremost a fortress. It is quite different with the castle Montargis, also dating from the beginning of the 13th century but not, as at Arques, as an extension of an older already existing castle, but as a new building (fig. 52). But even this could not prevent certain features of an older type living on within its structure. In the centre of the castle square there is a round tower with a central courtyard, a typical shell keep, but this does not contain all the rooms of the castle. Surrounding the tower there is a large courtyard with a number of buildings which serve different purposes such as meditation, ceremony and the changing demands of daily life, which remind us of the Imperial Palaces. In the eastern part of the castle square there is also the Great Hall—*la Grande Salle*—the most characteristic feature of a French Knight's castle. The surrounding wall is marked by closely spaced flanking towers, and the defence of the main gate is taken over by a donjon-like round tower. Even in the castle which Philippe Auguste erected in Paris as a predecessor to the Louvre, the donjon still occupied the place of honour. The Louvre, according to the

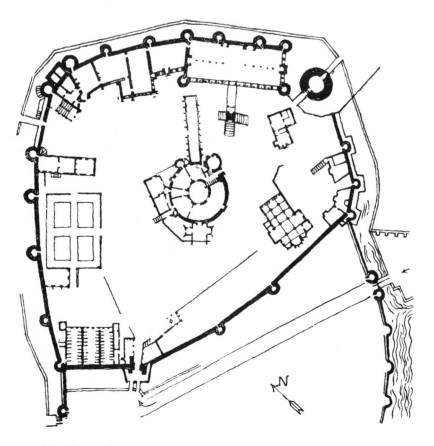

95 · Montargis, France

requirements of the time was only extended under Charles V (1364—80), and was originally destined only for military purposes, whilst the court life went on in the town palace on the Ile de la Cité. This palace was partly erected by Louis IX (with the famous Ste. Chapelle) and partly by Philippe le Bel, and is mainly representative of the exclusively residential building which had now broken away from military design.

During the first half of the 13th century, the power of the French nobility was still unbroken, and the feudal fortresses often grew into huge establishments. A symbol of all these is the well-known Coucy, which up to 1917 was still in fairly good repair (ill. 96, 97). The castle was built in the years 1225—30 on an existing structure and was already regarded in the Middle Ages as one of the most elegant in France. The motto of the owner also sounds self-confident: 'Roi ne suis, ne prince aussi. Je suis le Sire de Coucy'. The new style is expressed here quite clearly, without however shaking off all the old elements. A donjon still exists, not now alone but as *primus inter pares* of a well organised column of turrets. Admittedly, the master of the castle used the donjon occasionally as a dwelling and as a last refuge, but in time the

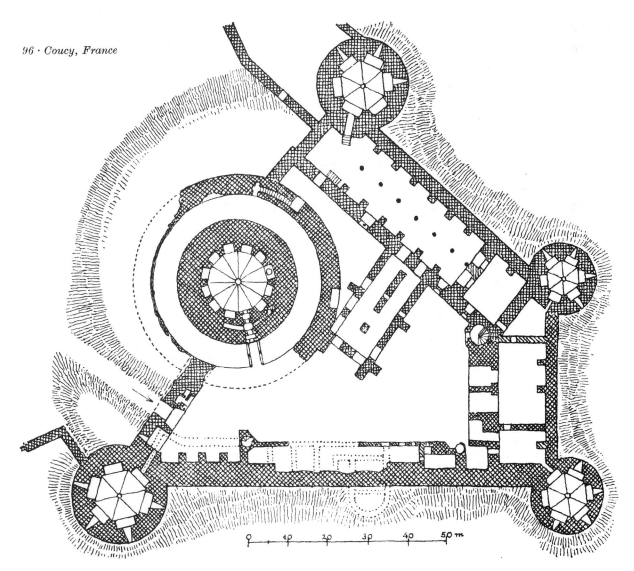

96 · Coucy, France

97 · Coucy, France: reconstruction

living rooms were moved out of the dark interior of the tower into the castle yard where
the strong surrounding walls permitted a new emphasis on its residential character. Here
there rises a church with large windows, a hall with wide-open arcades and with well
proportioned windows; in fact everything which could provide the knight with a worthy
frame for his cultural mode of life during the peak of the Middle Ages. Neither in France
nor elsewhere in the West is there a feudal castle that could compare with Coucy; in fact
it overshadows the fortresses of the German Emperor, and only England had something
similar to offer. On the same level of development stands the sprawling structure in Chinon
whose back portion—Château du Coudray—has, just like Coucy, on its attacking front
a donjon-like building which does not however differ much from the other towers (ill. 104).
Coucy represents the ultimate in private buildings in France. The power of the nobility
diminished from then on and in the second half of the 13th century the initiative passed

increasingly to the Crown and Church with the effect of following even more closely the definite Roman military style. In France a few Roman surrounding walls had remained whose existence must have been known, although the early Middle Ages on the whole ignored them. Only after the hard battles in Syria and Palestine where new siege methods and arms were employed, were these remains used. Probably the Crusades awakened an interest in the superior Arab defences, and, as already mentioned above, several details from their fortresses were incorporated. But when the new teachings found practical applications in the homeland, the local Roman remains which were also the basis of many Arab buildings in many cases served as a pattern. The town wall of Carcassonne is an instructive example (ill. 102, 103). The surrounding wall had been designed by the Romans and later extended by the West Goths in the 5th century; only in the 13th century was it completed in its present state. Although it was partly reconstructed, we obtain here a good picture of the surrounding wall, in its first phase, complete with round towers. The towers are still rather slender, the vertical defence is undeveloped, and the machicolated galleries, which were later typical, are missing. The gate is flanked on both sides by turrets. Here we have, in embryo, the characteristic French gate buildings which were becoming popular elsewhere in Northern Europe from the second half of the 13th century onwards. Another early example is the castle and town wall at Angers (ill. 107), which, seen as a whole, received its present shape in 1228—38, partly during the minority of Louis IX, when the Queen Mother, Blanche of Castille, energetically defended the work of Philippe Auguste.

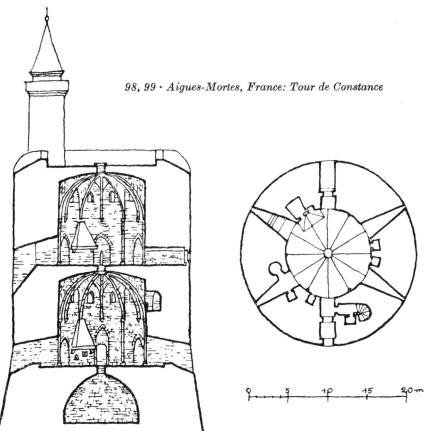

98, 99 · Aigues-Mortes, France: Tour de Constance

Much more advanced are the new military features at Aigues-Mortes which Louis IX in 1240 laid out as a French harbour on the Rhône delta and which was used as the chief base for both the Crusades led by him. Already in 1248, forty thousand crusaders foregathered there to depart for the East. In 1241—50 a tremendous round tower planned as a residence of the king, was erected (Tour de Constance, ill. 98, 99). The two interior rooms, forty feet high, with their fine Gothic vaults are still one of the most beautiful examples of the mature donjon architecture of the late Gothic period. Two-thirds of the way up the main room there runs a gallery built into the enormous thickness of the wall. The upper embattlement was rebuilt in the 17th century when the tower became a state prison. Only after Louis' death during the Crusade in 1270, was his son, Philippe le Bel, able to keep his father's promise to give the town a tremendous surrounding wall (ill. 105, 106). With its uniform long rectangular design, the town of Aigue-Mortes gives the impression of being a huge fortress of ancient times, and indeed the ruined Damietta in the Nile Delta is said to have been the model. The corners of the wall are protected by strong round towers and the gates which are placed at regular intervals in the steep street lie mostly in highly protective flanking positions; but the machicolation friezes are still missing. The vertical defence is assured by battlements which are situated in extensions or hidden in the wall. A part of them, however, must be regarded as closets with which the walls are fitted in large measure. Aigues-Mortes has one of the best preserved town walls of the Middle Ages; in fact it is not actually a town wall in the usual sense, but rather an encampment which stands, like an army column, in several formations, under the leadership of the king who is represented by the Tour de Constance at one corner. This interplay of donjon and castle layout is frequently met later in both France and England.

The 14th century continued the trend of the preceding hundred years. The donjon in modernised form appears as a bridge protection at Villeneuve-les-Avignon in the nobly

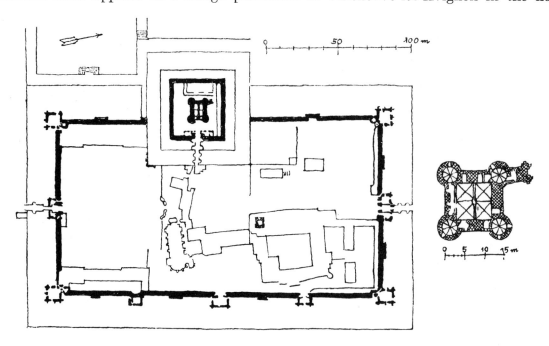

100 · *Vincennes, France*

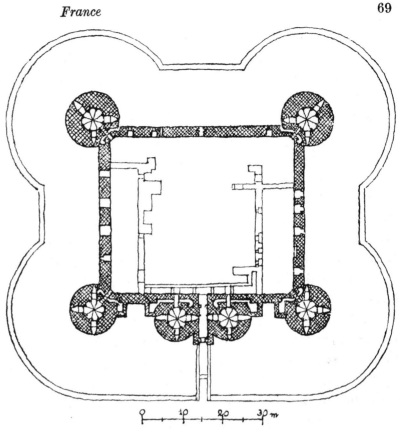

elegant Tower of Philippe le Bel completed in 1307. A considerable manifestation of the military style is to be found in the fortress of St. André in the same town which was erected in 1362—68 as a French outpost against the Papal town on the other side of the Rhône (ill. 108). This consists of an area surrounded by walls which serves exclusively as fortress so that the greatest emphasis lies on the defence of the gate. The French double gate design confronts us, fully perfected and with an effective and at the same time picturesque circle of battlements which crown the projecting wall masses. This gate design differs completely from the town wall around Avignon built by the Pope on the other side of the river, where Italian influence reveals itself. If one were to put Carcassone, Aigues-Mortes and St. André side by side, the rapid development of French fortress architecture would become apparent, springing from the same cultural soil in which a vast variety of cathedrals originated. The French fortress with its combination of residential and defence purposes is clearly demonstrated at Vincennes (ill. 100). Here the old and the new meet, for an encampment already existed in Vincennes at the time of Louis IX; after this the establishment was frequently extended, particularly under Charles V in the 1360's, who transformed Vincennes into a residential castle which consists of donjon and castle. The beautifully shaped donjon with its round corner turrets links up with older traditions. The castle line beside it is strictly regular and has four-cornered flanking towers, the corner towers of which can be likened to independent donjons. The mathematical exactitude of Vincennes invites comparison with a Roman castle which has been adapted to the requirements of the new age. The concept of the dwelling tower of the king and the encampment of his entourage can here best be compared with the same combination at Aigues-Mortes. At Vincennes, an ideal solution has been achieved from the point of view of fortification, in the manner in which the frontal, flanking and vertical protection has been arranged. Certain measures were also taken for protection against light firearms.

In the 13th century, the strictly regular fortress was the model even for the smaller establishments in which, hitherto, dwelling and military purposes were equally divided. The fortress of Villandraut (Gironde) built by Clement V (1306—07) is a frequently named example (ill. 101). The square fortress has round turrets, with two semi-circular towers flanking the entrance. Around the courtyard, there are three buildings against the surrounding wall which remind us of the Italian examples.

The same type of basic design also becomes apparent in the Louvre in Paris, in the form in which it was erected under Charles V. The old donjon was retained, the living quarters were grouped around the court and the surrounding walls were given corner turrets and gate buildings in the customary style of the 14th century. But the castle with closed living quarters around the court was not so stereotyped in France as in Italy. Beside the old donjon tradition, the emphasis on representative buildings lived on tenaciously. The castle of Pierrefonds (1390—1420) is an example of this (ill. 109, 117). The courtyard is surrounded on three sides only by narrow dwellings; situated on the entrance side there is a large house, which juts out, and resembles both the donjon and the hall-building. The fortress was built by the Duke of Valois in grandiose style, with huge halls and living rooms; but the most important suite of rooms for the Duke's dwelling was situated in the donjon-like main building where he could feel safer in time of danger. This arrangement, separating the lord of the castle from his retinue, is therefore to be regarded as a tradition which has been continued almost without interruption throughout the Middle Ages. One has only to look at the royal encampments of Aigues-Mortes and Vincennes. The fact that the arrangement of space in the French fortress designs was not influenced by the oriental courtyard house is even more clearly seen in smaller fortress buildings, for example, Sully-sur-Loire. The defence system here resembles Pierrefonds; on the court there is only one house as a main building containing two rooms which join smaller rooms on the entrance side (ill. 110).

The freer combination of various fortress elements is particularly noticeable in the architecture of the manor house. Frequently the main wall is absent, and the defences are combined with the main building. Often the manor houses are supplied with *échauguettes*, a French device of the 14th century which later became very popular in Northern Europe. At the strongest defence point, the gate tower was erected, not, as in the larger fortress buildings, with two semi-circular towers, but square ones, developments of the donjons. All these single elements are united in a typical manner in the Manor house at Xaintrailles (Lot-et-Garonne) which was built at the beginning of the 15th century (ill. 116).

About the year 1400, the division between defence and dwelling purposes becomes more pronounced still. It became increasingly difficult to bind these two elements together after the custom of the Middle Ages, particularly in the great Imperial residences. This dualism already appeared at the time of Pierrefonds, and similar conflicts are seen at Tarascon

102 · *Carcassonne, France: town wall*

103 · Carcassonne, France: gateway towers

104 · Chinon, France:
Château de Coudray

105 · Aigues-Mortes, France: town wall

106 · *Aigues-Mortes, France*

107 · *Angers, France: fortress*

108 · Villeneuve-les-Avignon, France: Fort St-André

109 · Pierrefonds, France

110 · Sully-sur-Loire, France

111 · Tarascon, France

112 · Beaucaire, France: donjon

113 · *Avignon, France: papal palace*

114 · *Avignon, France: Great Chapel of the papal palace*

115 · Mont-St-Michel, France

116 · *Xaintrailles, France: reconstruction*

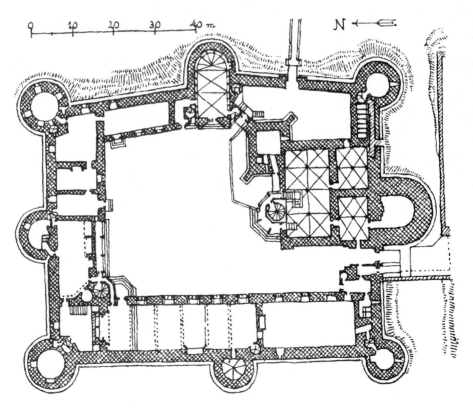

117 · *Pierrefonds, France*

in the royal fortress erected about 1400 (ill. 111). This complex of buildings, in parts
strongly overbuilt by restorations, is famous for its interior rooms with their emphasis on
habitability; and thus a representative monumental room is missing. The interior is
surrounded by a strong shell wall with turrets to the same height as the top of the wall,
so that the whole presents the aspect of a closed fortress of an extremely military design;
it is an outpost of the Imperial power on the Rhône. On the other side of the river, there is
the Romanesque Beaucaire with its triangular donjon dating from the 12th century which
was later raised and had the well-known French battlement gallery added to it (ill. 112). This
is a characteristic pair of fortresses. There are corresponding examples elsewhere, as in
Avignon, Narva-Ivangorod and Helsingborg. However, Beaucaire, with its peculiar triangular donjon, is unique among the solutions of the military elements of tower and wall.
Amongst these we may name the monumental Najac. In Perpignan, the Royal Palace of
the Kings of Mallorca has new restoration work which has above all brought out the artistic
effect of the interior rooms. Berzée, Crussol, Pilate and Rochemaure are known for their
beautiful situations. Southern France is also rich in military buildings such as the fortified
churches at Les Saintes-Maries-de-la-Mer, while the mills and bridges such as Pont Valentré
(Cahors) have a form which is reminiscent of Italian fortresses.

The Papal palace at Avignon occupies a special place in the military architecture of France
(ill. 113, 114, 118). It was created in the century of the 'Babylonian imprisonment' of the
Papacy, when Avignon took over the position of Rome and rose to the status of an international city with the seats of many Orders, the Cardinals' residences and the University.
This great complex was erected in 1316, and later extended in two stages, 1334—42, and
1342—52. The oldest part consists of a square of dwellings which are grouped around a larger
court of Italian pattern. Large halls are prevalent. The defence is taken care of by the square
towers and the loopholes in the crown of the building, and the pointed arches join the many
façades in a most monumental fashion and unite the different groups of buildings into a huge
complex. Particularily worthy of note is the huge dwelling tower erected by Pope Benedict XII
on the south side of the building. The newer part also consists of hall-like buildings surrounding a courtyard, even though they are not as close together as in the older one. The
south wing contains as its most elegant halls the large audience hall and the chapel, which
lie above each other; majestic creations of Gothic architecture (ill. 114). Here, Petrarch
and Simone Martini met. The Papal fortress must be regarded as one of the most important
fortresses of the 14th century. The example in the north corresponding to Avignon is to
be found in the main seat of the Grand Master of the German Order, the Marienburg in
Prussia. Not only in terms of size, but also in artistic construction, these are the greatest
secular buildings of the 14th century.

France's best-known cloister fortress lies in Normandy: Mont-St-Michel (ill. 115). The monastery was first constructed of stone in the 11th century, and church and military buildings were
added later at different periods. The integration of this most beautiful example of French Gothic
with a massive military construction produces a picture of impressive charm. From the picturesque cliff top of Mont-St-Michel, we can imagine ourselves transported into the Middle Ages.

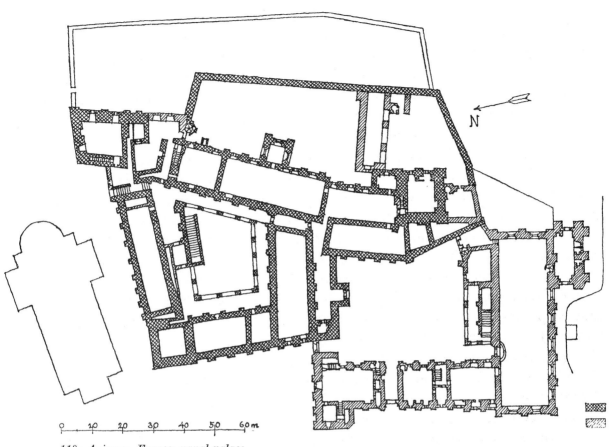

118 · Avignon, France: papal palace

SPAIN AND PORTUGAL

In Spain the battle of life and death between the Occident and the Orient had imposed its character on the fortress architecture of the country. It clearly reflects the hard and stern character of the Spanish knight and his obstinate fanaticism. From the middle of the eighth century a state of war was continuous for five hundred years; war between the small, Christian states of the mountainous regions of the North and the culturally superior invaders. When, in a later period, the frontier moved gradually southwards the Christians adopted the art of fortification as practised by the Moors. It must be remembered that more advanced methods of attack were employed in the battles of the Spanish wars than were then current in any other European country.

Spain's most noteworthy fortress of the early period is the town wall of Avila in old Castille (ill. 119). This is a granite wall, nearly two miles in length, with eighty-six identical turrets, and ten gates which are flanked by double towers. It was completed in 1090 by Raimond of Burgundy, the son-in-law of Alfonso VI of Leon and Castille. According to one version it was begun in 1088 and designed by the Italian Cassandro and the Frenchman, Florian de Ponthieu, and completed by twelve 'Masters of Geometry' who supervised the Spanish workmen. The contribution of the Italian Cassandro was probably decisive. The city wall of Avila appears in comparison with Western fortress architecture of the time to be a strange anachronism, which has a parallel only in the France of the 13th century.

In all other respects the contact with France was a close one, the French Crusader armies taking part in the battles against the Arabs. At the same time in Burgundian Cluny the Benedictines organized a pilgrimage to the supposed grave of the apostle James, at Santiago de Compostella, and French warriors and monks took part. Christian Spain was made a province of Cluny and the nobility consisted of immigrant French knights. This affected even the fortress architecture, particularly in the introduction of the donjon. One is, nevertheless, reminded of the older tradition of the country and of her contact with the Arab world. The tower fortress was, in most cases, a watch tower, such as the simple square one at Aledo or the round one at La Rabita. The chief accent was on defence. Some of these buildings can be traced back to pre-Medieval structures. During the period of the intense battles for power in the 15th century between king and nobles, the tower was replaced by a large composite structure and grew in dimensions, just as it did in France. The tower fortress was now combined with the French round tower system which contrasted with the older Moorish development and its square flanking towers. Fuensaldaña, built in 1500, has round corner towers in the style of Vincennes (ill. 120). In accordance with long established custom the tower is reached through a door situated high up and leading to a suspension bridge. Next to the tower there is a castle which is designed to take the domestic rooms. This design looks like a Roman desert castle in its proud seclusion. Such a combination of tower and castle is typical of Spain. Another example worthy of mention is the Alcazar of Segovia whose older parts date from the 13th century. During the 15th century the construction was extended and in the 19th it underwent a rather misguided restoration. In the same category may be included the fortress of La Mota (Medina del Campo), Guardamur, Arenas de San Pedro, Peñafiel and many other buildings mostly from the 14th and 15th centuries. There are, however, castles without a prominent donjon. The fortress of Alacuas is a block of buildings in the form of a closed cube, with square corner towers, which reminds us of an Italian Palace. In the middle is an inner courtyard-patio with archways leading to the large halls of the fortress where the rich ornamentation stands in stark contrast to the severe exterior. It is often the interior of the fortress where Arab motifs are most predominant. Alcalá de Guadaira has massive square towers, probably built by the Moors. The fact that rectangular towers were particularly popular with the Moors is borne out by the famous Alhambra, a combination of palace and fortress. The large palace area is protected by a defence-wall, still standing, with projecting square turrets which are however furnished as a kind of summer abode. Only one single tower (Alcazaba) takes over the defence and could be held even after the other parts had fallen.

Several castles with massive round corner turrets and battlement friezes are based on French examples. To this category belong Maqueda and Perelada, the latter rebuilt in modern times (ill. 121). Manzanares del Real (1435) is also French in its fortification system, whereas in decoration it contains typically Spanish traits. Even more strongly characteristic is the wealth of detail of the Spanish late-Gothic, to be seen in the fortress Coca (Segovia)

119 · Avila, Spain: town wall

120 · *Fuensaldaña, Spain*

121 · *Perelada, Spain*

122 · Castillo de Coca, Spain

123 · *Amieira, Portugal*

124 · *Lisbon: fortress*

which was built entirely from brick and whose defence system incorporated varying kinds of ramparts and wall towers (ill. 122). The design consists of a court-patio surrounded by four small wing buildings. Here too the typical Spanish donjon has been introduced into the fortress, the feudal tower which forms a fortification in itself. Around the fortress there is a strong wall, with corner towers which have peculiarly shaped bases like pencil points and which are rich in decoration. Such a wealth of different designs is exceptional however. As a rule the Spanish fortress maintains its serious character throughout the Middle Ages. During the late Middle Ages the military severity received even greater emphasis due to the wars between the nobility and the kings from which the royal power emerged strengthened.

As well as the citadel and tower fortress Spain has beautiful examples of fortresses conforming to the terrain, situated on precipitous cliffs. Frequently these fortresses are older than the citadels and not infrequently the old Arab foundations have been used, as for example in Alcazaba (Almeria), where the surrounding walls with square turrets parallel certain features of Byzantine Arab fortresses in Syria. The cliff fortress Santa Barbara in Alicante was built under Roman rule. Later, the Moors took over the buildings of fortresses and in the year 1301 the city was conquered by Ferdinand III. The buildings rise like crystals from the steep cliff tops of Jativa; here also the square turrets speak of their Arab heritage.

Portugal is one of the countries of Europe richest in fortresses. Influences from Arab fortress architecture can be felt and thus the fortresses of Portugal have also shared in some of the heritage of Roman times. Some of the buildings can be traced back to the time of the independence of the country, but most of them have either been completely rebuilt or newly constructed after breaking away from Castille. There was much building activity during the critical period from about 1170 up to the beginning of the 13th century, in other words, during the time of the first stirrings of independence when the Alentejo plains were conquered and the borders of the country were defined. A Moorish invasion was still threatening, and there was also the danger of war with Castille. In the southern part of the Tejo Plain a number of fortresses were constructed which were to prevent any possible enemy attack.

The tower-castle and citadel are leading types in Portugal, and just as in Spain the feudal tower appears in varying forms. We find the latter standing in solitary domination, as in Braganza, one of the largest fortifications in Portugal, the older parts of which were begun in 1187. But even in the pure citadel type the donjon occurs, for example in Amieira (ill. 123) which was built in the second half of the 14th century by Alvaro Concalves Pereia, the Prior of the Hospital Order. At last, it was with the help of the Knights of St. John and Knights Templar who were called in, that Portugal was extended, and they left their mark on the fortress architecture. Actually, in fortresses of the type of Amieira, much survives of the architecture which had its roots in Syria and which extended in various guises throughout southern Italy and the countries of the Teutonic Order. The design consists of a quadrangle with rectangular towers on each corner of which the one at the entrance is the main tower of the fortress. This is a later version of a military castle of ancient Arab design and the poorly planned design of the cloister fortress distinguishes itself clearly in the North European dwelling constructions. The fortress at Lisbon belongs to the same category. In its regular straight silhouette which partly originates from the Saracen fortress conquered in 1147 by Alfonso Henriques (ill. 124), a donjon has been added to the main wall. A certain similarity with some Italian city fortresses is noticeable. On the whole, the character here is far more military than in Italy. Of this basic design, many stately fortresses such as Trancosa, Pombal, Montemor-o-Velho, Obidos and Silves may be mentioned. Square turrets predominate; where there are round flanking turrets French influence is indicated. In interior decoration, the church is sometimes superior (Viana do Alentejo).

BRITISH ISLES

Three sources influenced English military architecture of the late Middle Ages: the old local building traditions, the experience of the Crusaders and French architecture. But, as in ecclesiastical, so also in fortress architecture, all foreign elements were transformed by a strong *genius loci*.

Even in Romanesque times, in addition to the keep, the surrounding wall was in use, but not many flanking towers, although there are examples of such designs preserved from the Roman period (Porchester, ill. 13). The surrounding walls either ran regularly or followed the circular shape of the motte design; in both cases they only had small wall projections which did not possess any particular flanking towers. The defence moreover was frontal. From the end of the 12th century surrounding walls were built with turrets; for instance Framlingham (Suffolk) in the years 1190—1200 received its defence belt with projecting rectangular turrets. During the 3rd Crusade (1189), knowledge of Byzantine fortress buildings was acquired from the multi-terraced walls of Constantinople, and this seems to have impressed the master builder of Framlingham. Arab buildings in which the square turret predominated were also seen in Syria. The interior wall at Dover may be included in the same category as Framlingham. (ill. 129). However, the square turret was only retained for a short period, and was then quickly changed for the system with semi-circular or circular turrets. At the peak of this development, the British adopted the D-shape in their basic design in order to offer more space for defenders. The earliest round towers are to be seen at Conisborough; later they followed in Skenfrith (Monmouthshire) and Pevensey (Sussex), the latter dated about 1250 with particularly strong D-shaped turrets. The Tower of London also then received its wall belt with the round towers characteristic of this time.

Associated with the constant increase in architectural activity in the second half of the 13th century is the production of the typical English fortress. A peak was reached under Edward I (1272—1307), a soldier-king who had had much battle experience from the Crusade of 1271—1272 in Syria, the conquest of Wales in 1288, and battles against the Scots. These experiences, with a new impetus from Syria and France, resulted in the concentric fortress: that is, a construction comprising several defence lines and a combination of single turrets and walls in a well-balanced unity. The fortress could only be conquered step by step. Every turret could resist individually even when the fortress as a whole had already surrendered. A large number of huge constructions were started by Edward I, and continued by his son Edward II (1307—1327) as well as his grandson Edward III (1327—1377). These Plantagenet fortresses leave their mark over a period of more than a hundred years, a period of battles and lust for power, of conquest and defeat. The fortress of Flint, built in 1277

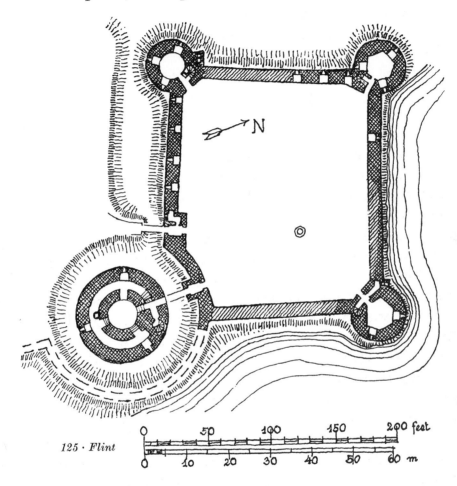

125 · Flint

(ill. 125), is one of the first constructions of the time of Edward I. The French elements are particularly apparent here; the donjon placed in one corner is rather reminiscent of Coucy as well as of the Tour de Constance at Aigues-Mortes. Here also, the corner turrets and the basic design show French influence. They are not direct copies of these models, but the manner in which the Flint keep had been combined with the castle-fortress is fairly uncommon. Even before the reign of Edward I, Caerphilly Castle was started in 1267, which, when completed ten years later, was England's largest fortress (ill. 128). The basic design is typically concentric, with double wall belts, massive corner towers and gates, which with their D-shaped towers, portcullis and drawbridges form small fortresses in themselves. The military purpose overshadows everything, the habitable part consists merely of one hall and some dwellings on the southern side of the fortress court. To the east and west of the main fortress, strongly built projections were added.

In the 1280's this stylistic direction reaches a peak with the fortresses of Conway, Caernarvon and Harlech. Of rectangular plan, the powerful Conway rises on a hill, the surrounding wall picketed closely with strong round towers. Some of these are crowned with slender watch turrets in order to follow the operations of the enemy in the vicinity of the fortress (ill. 130). The massive effect is the same as in the Crusader fortresses of Syria. The construction is divided into two, with a castle-like main fortress with royal lodge as well as a projection in which the typically English hall is situated. The gates to the east and west lack D-shaped turrets, but each contains a barbican. In its basic design, Conway comes very close to Caernarvon (ill. 131); even the architecture is comparable and it is supposed that they had the same builder. Caernarvon is counted among the most beautiful fortresses of Edward I. The whole construction has a stern military character. Not only has the basic design been worked out with great precision, but the walls, the octagonal turrets crowned by small watch towers and the defence system of the gates are marked by a feeling for style which was based on military requirements and the need for architectural precision. Of the towers, the Eagle Tower to the west is the largest and has all the characteristics of a keep, from which the whole fortress was commanded. The tower also contains a small chapel and, on the ground floor, a small sallyport. The turrets and walls have been extremely well preserved and are rich in military details. Conway and Caernarvon must be counted as the most beautiful fortresses of their kind ever to have been constructed in the Occident, and among the largest. Only Coucy and Angers can be compared with them.

Among the Plantagenet fortresses are Harlech (1283—1290) and Beaumaris (1295—1323), representative of the strong castle type, upon which Caerphilly was modelled (ill. 126, 127, 132). Both are surrounded by double defence works and with the exterior position of the round towers all the rules of the flanking system have been observed. The gate-houses with D-shaped double turrets form independent defence points with ample space. The other towers are also strong enough to offer stiff independent resistance to an attacker. Beaumaris, particularly, is an example of the perfect military fortress of the time before the rise of firearms. The whole defence system was so well planned that the fortress could be manned by a fairly small garrison.

English fortress architecture was at its peak during the time of the Edwards. Those castles that were built later cannot be compared with fortresses of the type of Conway, Harlech, Caernarvon, Caerphilly, etc., the gigantic buildings of the last quarter of the 13th century and the beginning of the 14th. In the 14th century fewer castles were built, their military function was less accentuated and dwelling places became more and more separated. A typical one is Nunney, founded in 1373 (ill. 133). In comparison with other constructions of the period, Nunney is a miniature fortress, and is reminiscent of the keep, where the corner turrets have taken over the main defence. The four massive round towers remind us of French fortresses; the vertical protection by means of battlements is now complete as the well-preserved corbels prove. Presumably a French master builder was in charge at Nunney, and it has been supposed that the Bastille in Paris was its prototype. The Bastille was a purely military construction. Nunney may be regarded as the last refuge castle, linking up

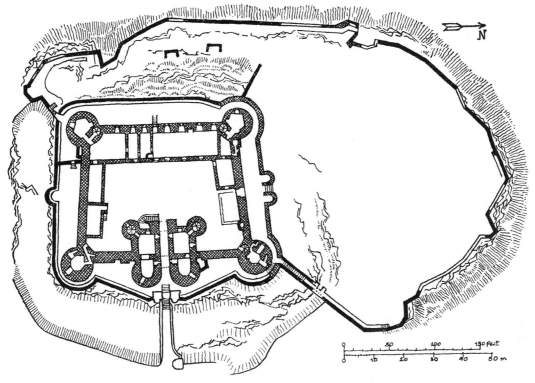

126 · Harlech

the old military principles with a new shape, a solution which we meet in several forms later.

The conflict between military and dwelling purposes in England during the late Middle Ages is noticeable in varying ways. It was desired as far as possible to adapt the fortress to the new defence requirements. At the same time the necessity for reasonable living conditions had to be considered. Bodiam, started in 1386 and completed in the 1390s is a vivid example of this dual purpose (ill. 134). The basic design is square and the defence is concentrated into four round corner turrets and as many square turrets lying in between. Their entrances are to the north and south and a complicated structure covers the entrance. The living quarters are situated in wings, generally narrow, round a court, and there are windows in the exterior walls which give the fortress a much more peaceful character than was the case in the constructions of the 13th century. In its basic design Bodiam resembles the fortresses of the 14th century in France, as for example Villandraut and the Louvre, but stronger similarities with the type of fortress introduced by Frederick II in Sicily may be seen. Bodiam, as a type, won great popularity in the late Middle Ages (Maxtoke, Bolton, Lumley, Chillingham), even if it did not fulfil all defence requirements. There was, for example, no specially isolated part in the interior of the fortress which could serve as a last refuge in the event of the enemy succeeding in entering the walls. Thus, the old keep was again introduced into a number of combined constructions, which rather resemble Pierrefonds, in France.

This tendency leads consequently to a revival of the keep. But regarded from the viewpoint of life within a fortress, the keeps were used differently from those of Romanesque times.

The epoch of the Knights had passed, the Lord of the Castle no longer had only sympathetic brothers-in-arms in his service; he now also had professional soldiers, who sold themselves to any leader. Mutinies against authority often occurred, particularly during wars against France, and the lord of the castle felt safer within his family tower or in some other isolated part of the construction. This contributed to the fact that also in other large military designs, such as Harlech, the gate-houses were furnished as the living-quarters of the lord, since even in the event of disunity amongst the fortress garrison, it would be difficult to conquer. Similar constructions from the late Middle Ages illustrate how the keep once again occupied its place of honour, and this, apart from purely practical reasons, was also to symbolise the power of the lord of the fortress. Thus at Warkworth (Northumberland), built in about 1390, the dwelling tower stands completely isolated from all the other buildings. Warkworth, in its perfect design, is unique in England. On each side of the square centre tower there are semi-octagonal projections which give the building the shape of a cross. The tower contains, amongst other things, a large hall, and a chapel, which are known for

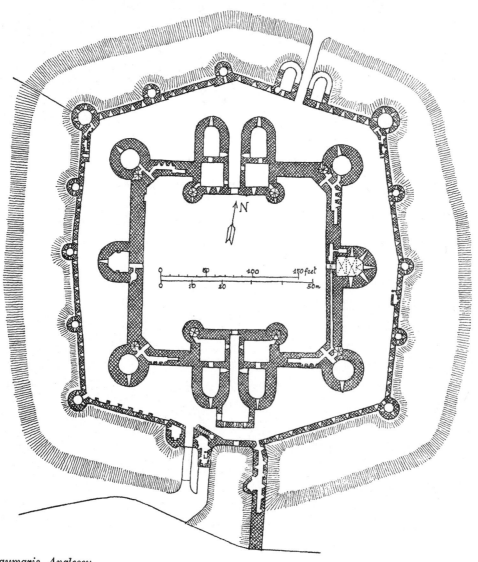

127 · Beaumaris, Anglesey

128 · Caerphilly

129 · Dover

130 · Conway

131 · Caernarvon

132 · *Harlech*

133 · Nunney

134 · Bodiam, Sussex

135 · *Tattershall, Lincolnshire*

136 · *Winchester: Great Hall*

137 · Crichton, Scotland

138 · Bothwell, Scotland

139 · Coxton, Scotland

140 · *Trim, Ireland*

141 · Carrickfergus, Ireland

142 · Blarney

their beautiful architecture. The Tattershall tower (1431—1439) is more traditional. From this a direct line can be traced to the Norman keep (ill. 135). The tower, on the west side of a fortress court of the 13th century, is built of brick. Even up to the first half of the 15th century English fortresses were built exclusively of brown stone.

Not all English fortresses can be classified. The architectural history of several large and important fortresses stretches from the days of the Normans to the end of the Middle Ages. Every century contributed something new. At Windsor, for instance, there is a Norman shell keep in Gothic form in the centre and on both sides a stretch of castle grounds, with buildings in the best English Gothic style. Another magnificent example is Warwick, with its façade of hundreds of windows. It is closely in keeping with the English character that the traditional forms are stubbornly kept alive. Ashby-de-la-Zouche (1463—1481) has been called the last great English fortress of the Middle Ages. This building consists of a number of houses picturesquely grouped, with a military keep, and a traditional hall in the centre of the living quarters. One hardly need add that in almost all fortresses the hall was given a place of honour, where the interior architecture of the English Gothic style could blossom freely under the protection of the strong surrounding walls (Winchester, ill. 136).

In Scotland fortress architecture first blossomed with the feudalization of the south Scottish nobility in the reign of David I (1124—1153). The development is not quite so spasmodic as in the days of William the Conqueror, but the old military constructions develop slowly under the feudal system. For a long time, constructions were of wood, and it was only in the 13th century that stone was used in greater quantity as building material. The flanking system may first be seen at Dirleton (East Lothian), a fortress which belonged to the De Vaux family, and the older parts of which originate from around 1225. But it was only towards the end of the 13th century and the beginning of the 14th that the new defence system became more widespread, as a result of hard fought battles with the English which often took place around the large fortresses such as Bothwell, Caerlaverock and Kildrummy. At Bothwell, the chief emphasis is on a round corner turret of the castle in a similar style to the turrets to be found at Coucy and Flint (ill. 138). Part of the main tower at Bothwell originates from the end of the 13th century, the rest of the construction being added later, as at Caerlaverock and Kildrummy. The former (ill. 143) boasts an imposing gate-house in the style of the Edwardian fortresses. The design as a whole, however, is triangular which directly recalls the Castello di Sarzanello north of Pisa (ill. 219), which was built about 1325. Kildrummy also had a basic design resembling a triangle. The concentric system here too has been adapted to local conditions.

From the second half of the 14th century building activity increased, until its culmination in the 15th century. The nobility had won a very powerful position, and the desire for comfort grew. But the constant strife between the clans never allowed the defence interests to lie dormant. In the larger constructions these two components were now linked in a manner typical of Scotland. In these palace-fortresses the defence was taken over by a strong dwelling tower, and the comfort by a large palace which was often equipped with unusual splendour.

In many cases fortresses of this period grew into large complex buildings which combined the tower and other buildings in the same way and at the same time as in England and France, for example the coastal fortress at Dunottar, Crichton (ill. 137). The tower, however, became the most popular form of building amongst the lower nobility. Such dwelling towers in various forms exist, and their significance outlasted the Middle Ages (Coxton, ill. 139). The 14th century towers are usually simple, with only one room in each storey, and wide niches for windows, with small side rooms in the thickness of the wall. In time, however, the trend towards comfort grew and several towers were united in one complex building, which usually contained one common staircase. In these small fortresses, with their calculated simplicity and technical correctness, the Scottish characteristics are clearly expressed, in particular, in the old solid hewn-stone technique of the very popular decorative protruding turrets and the richly graduated corbel friezes of the exterior walls.

A group in itself consists of the small defence towers, which were built in the border regions and served as watch towers and refuges in uneasy times. Several of these border fortresses are preserved, for example, Amisfield, and seem like late mediaeval variants of the Roman *burgi*, perhaps like those originally on Hadrian's wall. The *burgi*, however, faced north, whereas the border fortresses protect themselves from danger from the south.

The conquest of Ireland by the Normans, masters of fortress architecture, in the second half of the 12th century meant the introduction of feudalism and despotism, based naturally

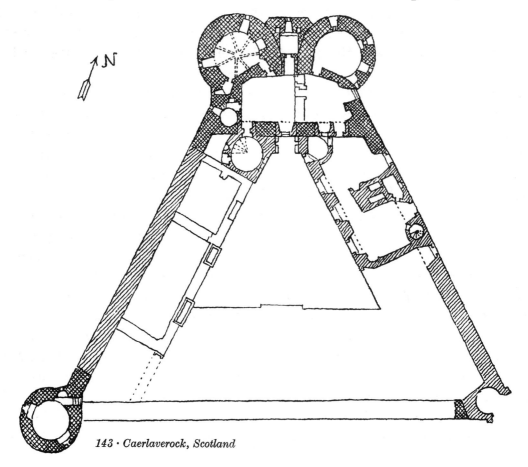

143 · *Caerlaverock, Scotland*

on a system of fortresses. The tower fortress was the earliest type. The central tower at Carrickfergus was built about 1200 and is related to tall rectangular keeps at Rochester and in other parts of England (ill. 141). Round this tower was later added a wall with a strong double gate. One notable tower fortress is Trim, which was built in the early 13th century on an ancient fortress site (ill. 140). The building is in the shape of a cross, and can therefore be compared to Warkworth in England. As at Carrickfergus, the outer wall belt at Trim was later extended, as the fortress had to protect an important crossing on the river Boyne. Proof that this type was popular is provided by the fortress of Rushen on the Isle of Man, where the actual tower in the centre probably originated in the 12th century and the arms of the cross were added later.

With the Anglo-Norman influence, the flanking tower became known, for example at Limerick, which was conquered by the Normans in 1195, and was in 1226 still in the possession of the English king. Roscommon is probably the purest type of concentric fortress of the second half of the same century. The basic design is quite regular, the corners have D-shaped turrets and the gate designs are very similar to corresponding designs at Harlech, Beaumaris and in the Plantagenet castles. Roughly the same type is also seen at Ballymote, also built in the second half of the 13th Cange. A large number of other fortresses could be listed as further proof of the general spread of the round tower in Ireland during the 13th century. There are also military constructions, without special accent on the tower, as in the case particularly of the fortified monasteries, some of these (Athassel) being block-like buildings, which remind one of Germanic fortresses. But no one type of fortress predominated as was the case, for instance, in the Low Countries and on the lower Rhine.

The construction of large fortresses did not appeal to the Irish, and in consequence, a long interval occurred after the building of the Anglo-Norman fortresses. Besides this, revolutions raged in the 14th century, and reduced the country to anarchy. In the 15th century the situation became moderately stabilised, but even then the country was a home of true warriors, most of whom served in the Hundred Years War. From the end of the 15th century onwards, there came a new wave of military building. And now the tower fortress became a symbol of the defeat of the Irish nobility up to the 17th century (Blarney, ill. 142). Naturally, foreign influence was strong, but at the same time local features may clearly be recognised. Most of the tower fortresses of the late Middle Ages are square, often tapering towards the top (Jerrycarrig Castle). The interior of the tower shows the same individual features as in Scotland, with a preference for wall niches and small side-rooms in the thickness of the walls. Occasionally the tower is surrounded by a wall which either runs round a court with side-buildings or is drawn closely around the tower as a mantel-wall (Fiddaun). Hanging-towers did not occur as frequently as in Scotland. On the other hand, vertical protection by means of structures in front of the gate buildings is fairly common. All these things are included but in a style of their own, which results in a certain local tradition in spite of foreign influence. The total impression is hard and warlike. From the situation of the fortresses we may recognise their strategic and economic role. The country's wealth of lakes and moors was skilfully made use of, in order to bar the most important entrances from attack by invaders and rivals for power, a characteristic which is already notable in the numerous prehistoric earthworks. Bridge fortresses have not infrequently grown into impressive buildings in themselves (Bunratty).

GERMANY

Nowhere in Europe does fortress architecture present such a varied picture as in Germany and the border regions coming under her influence. Germany's map of fortresses is just as complicated as the rest of its geography. It consists of small states each of which has its own characteristics. Within the framework of a list of western fortresses, it becomes impossible to class the German group as one entity. Also this is not really necessary if one regards the topic from the point of view of general military principles. However picturesque the fortresses situated on the peaks may appear, however complicated their basic design may be, the constructions may nevertheless be divided up by reason of their most important military elements and living quarters into a number of clearly defined principal types. Just as in the first half of the Middle Ages, so now, the main groups may also be divided into those having wall-protection adapted to natural local features, and the central defence system allied to the tower and the castle.

Of these categories, the first—a wall closely adapted to the terrain—is the most important and most characteristic of late medieval German fortress architecture. As already noted above, these adaptations to surrounding terrain are not only dependent on the availability of suitable mountain peaks; varying factors have contributed to the fact that a great number of German fortresses are adapted to nature. An important role in this is played also by the social and political conditions in Germany at this time, which differed considerably from those of other countries. In Italy most of the stylish fortresses were situated in the cities. Apart from this, the southern part of the country, at the time when the Gothic fortresses were built, was ruled by a central power, as was the case in France and England with their enormous military constructions of the 13th century. There the creations of man did not take any great advantage of the help offered by nature. Also the Roman-Oriental type could influence the development without hindrance. In Germany it was different. There the courts of the many rulers lay scattered and lonely all over the country. Fortresses arose close to them after old Germanic custom. Everywhere that the political and strategic situation called for military construction, the fortresses arose, in forest and mountain districts, near waterways, high roads, and imperial borders, not only in order to rule the country lawfully and economically, but also in an endeavour to dominate the landscape. Frederick Barbarossa constantly stressed this purely artistic dominance of fortress architecture. During the time of the Hohenstaufen the German fortress underwent its greatest development, stagnating later on in the first half of the 13th century. The splendid era of the Emperor's power had slipped by. During the interregnum of 1254—1273, there arose various small territories. Now the fortresses were no longer co-ordinated posts under the Emperor's jurisdiction, but frequently were dangerous bastions of powerful individuals, sometimes bandits (W. Hotz). The initiative passed more and more into the hands of the lower nobility and the fortress was re-shaped as a private dwelling, often characterised purely by considerations of usefulness. It was sought, if possible, to utilise such territorial formations which would best contribute to defence, and which would require the least labour. In this way, fortress and cliff were more firmly combined than ever.

Germany now showed a preference for that type of castle which was erected on a jutting mountain-peak, and which was separated by a moat from the rest of the mountain plateau. The main fortification for defence was a wall-belt. Such castles were frequently rebuilt as flanking towers became popular, for example Salzburg, which was probably founded in 1200 on the site of an older military establishment (ill. 144). The outer walls generally follow the edge of the mountain; in the north east there is a typical border-wall strengthened by small turrets covering the flanks. It is these towers which, in Germany, mark the first contact with Syrian-French buildings and designs. Covering the flank necessitated straight walls, even if, at the same time, it was desirable to follow the irregularities of the ground.

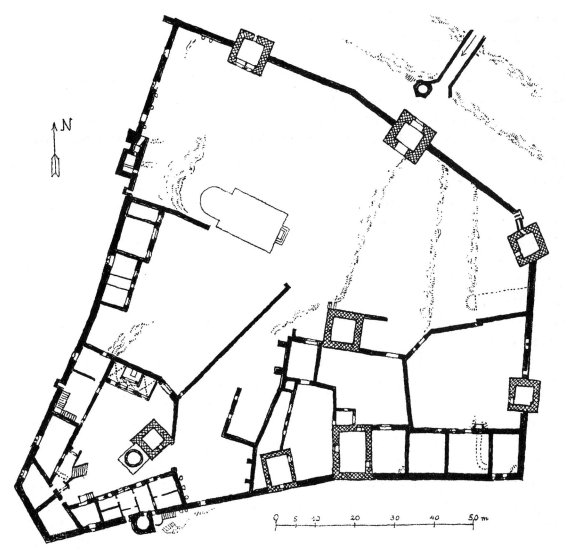

144 · Salzburg, Germany

Smaller buildings lay in picturesque disorder about the large courtyard. Salzburg was designed to be occupied by several families, and this had an effect on the arrangement of the living quarters. In contrast to the small number of buildings on the forecourt of Roman times, most of the Gothic constructions have many.

A variation of this type of castle was the fortress with a mantle-wall high on the front from which danger was most likely to come, which was occasionally built with one or more towers. This type had already been known in Romanesque times, but continued roughly up to the 14th century, and was revived in a changed form on the introduction of firearms. The example most often cited is Ortenberg in Alsace, which dates from the 13th century, where the mantle-wall is combined with the mountain refuges. In accordance with the general tendency of development the 'bergfrieds' were later dispensed with on the main front which was protected only by a mantle-wall instead, as, for instance in Schönburg on the Rhine (ill. 148), or Runkel on the river Lahn.

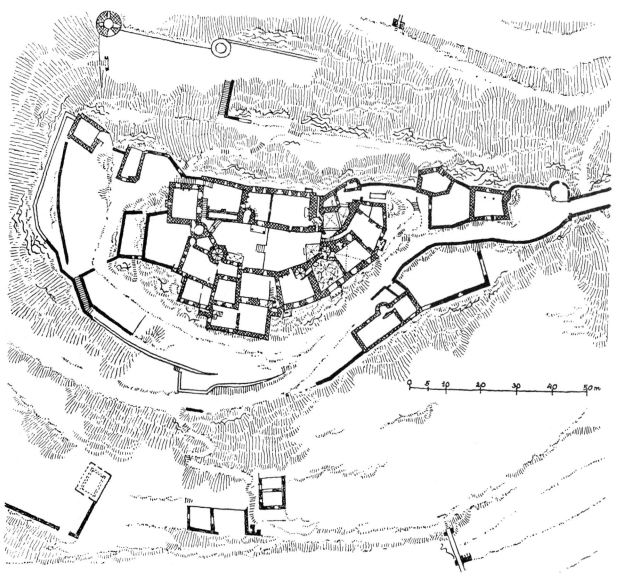

145 · *Eltz, Germany*

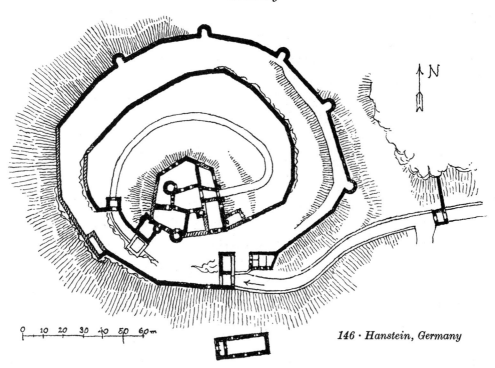

146 · Hanstein, Germany

When the fortress was situated on a hill or conical mountain which had to be protected equally effectively on all sides, either the well-tried type with a central tower was chosen or the main emphasis was laid on the buildings surrounding the fortress court, a category called *randhausburgen* (literally 'surrounding-house-castles'). One of the most beautiful fortresses of this kind is Eltz on the Moselle, a building which has become one of the proto-types of German fortress architecture (ill. 145, 149). Eltz is also a fortress for several families, and was extended in various building periods from the 12th to the 16th century. A Rudolf Elce is mentioned as owner in 1157, and from then onwards up to our times the fortress belonged to the same family. The main body of the building has grown up piece by piece like a bird's nest. The oldest part consists of the Plattelz tower from the 12th and 13th centuries; the other parts of the building contain beautiful interiors from the 15th century, with an appearance influenced by urban culture (ill. 150). The contrast is considerable if one thinks of the French Halls of the Knights, and the English halls.

However, German fortresses do not lack larger rooms, particularly in royal palaces. The Great Hall of the Marburger castle was influenced a little by the French style. It was the residence of the Landgrafs of Thuringia and Hesse (ill. 151, 153). The wide arched and pillared hall dates from the beginning of the 14th century. The fortress came into existence in stages. The oldest parts originate from the early Middle Ages, but the actual defences were later thoroughly overhauled, and the tall manor-house which contains a small chapel in select Gothic style as well as the Hall became a landmark of the Lahn valley.

Practically all large Romanesque fortresses were supplemented in the late Middle Ages, in order to incorporate the flanking principle as much as possible. As a rule, a process was followed in which an older fortress was surrounded by a wall covered by flanking turrets,

147 · Marksburg, Germany: reconstruction

thus automatically forming a new fortress. However, the flanking principle was not carried out quite so consistently as in France and England. On the other hand, the old German fortress system was of various types not to be found among the fortresses of these countries. We have already mentioned Münzenberg as an example (ill. 62), but even there, where the fortress was erected at the same time as the walls, the basic design often follows the same principle, as also at Hanstein in Hessen, erected in 1308 (ill. 146). Such buildings have as much right to be called 'concentric' as of the concentric fortresses in England, although the main role here has not been given to the turrets but to the walls. This architectural device gave effective protection against the enemy, and helped to prevent mining attempts and the erection of war machines. It is not as improbable as it sounds, when popular tradition tells us that bears and dogs were kept in the fortress gates; the name 'Bären-zwinger' (bear-keeps) is derived from this.

In all German landscapes, there are examples of fortresses following the terrain which were nearly all extended and completed at different periods. Particularly famous from prehistoric times for its beautiful scenery is the Rhine Valley; it is equally famous for its fortresses and fortress ruins, which, more than anywhere else, have become part of the landscape.

A classic example is found in the Marksburg near Braubach, whose central tower originates from Romanesque times (ill. 147, 152). The military devices around this tower have grown up gradually. The fortress forms a collective whole, however, and at the same time, seems to be a continuation of the mountain on which it stands. Just like Eltz, the Marksburg contains small homely rooms, even though they bear the resounding name Hall of the Knights. The fortress was carefully restored under Bodo Ebhardt. On the outside there are the small hanging turrets of French origin, and the arched friezes, typical in the Rhineland, extend above the massive walls of the fortress. Other fortresses, however, under the stress of different conditions, have more warlike characteristics, as is proved by the fortresses in the Upper Palatinate which were exposed to heavy battles. These are often strong buildings, closed in after the Romanesque style: for example, Obermurach, Prunn in Altmühltal (ill. 155) rebuilt in the 17th century.

Century after century contributed to the building of the Marien fortress in Würzburg, the seat of the Archbishops who reigned as country gentry in Franconia. On the fortress-court stands the famous pre-Romanesque round chapel, in isolation, near the 'bergfried'. In the Scharenberg fortress of the south front (1482), the attacking forces of the Peasant Wars came to a halt. The Pappenheim fortress in the Altmühl valley also displays a meticulously worked out fortress system, which could only be penetrated by the Swedes at the third attempt. In Upper Bavaria there is the border fortress of Burghausen on the river Salzach, one of the largest fortresses in Germany. This huge building, built as protection against the Turks, which stretches along more than 1,000 yards on a mountain top and is divided up into six castles, originated mainly from 1479 to 1503.

In central Germany, a notable fortress is Coburg with its protective belt which is fully adapted to the terrain (ill. 154). The rooms are completely altered. As with Coburg, many other fortresses in Thuringia and Hesse have been extended. There was little new building here in the late Middle Ages. Compared to the Rhineland, Saxony is poor in fortresses, if one disregards the fortresses on the Saale which have been renovated many times. Of large buildings, Elsterberg shows versatility, with robust fortress walls and flanking turrets. Further in the east, Silesia, Bohemia and Moravia possess composite types of German style (Bolkoburg, Kynast).

In the largest part of these German fortresses, the daily life has a decisive effect on the distribution of the rooms. The fortress consisted mostly of smaller rooms, houses divided into two, and turret-like buildings which were dotted about irregularly without a clear basic design. But as already shown, in Eltz, Marburg and Marksburg, even within this narrow scope the architectural trend of the Gothic period could effectively create stylistically pure interiors, frequently more individual and appealing than the great purely military fortresses. One should discard any idea that the legendary halo which in the 19th century used to surround the age of Knighthood was reflected in everyday life, for life in most of the fortresses was hard, commonplace and very much dependent on the climate and other natural elements. As a rule only one room could be heated: the women's quarters (*camera caminata*). Apart from this, window glass was not widely used before the 15th century.

The rooms were damp and dark, and the spring was impatiently awaited to drive away the long dark winter. In comparison with our times when technical knowledge helps us to replace the light and warmth of the sun, life was very much more conditioned by Nature.

The rectangular castle of the period does not occupy the same place as in Italy, France and England. This may be due to the more private character of the fortress architecture which needed no large military constructions. The only exceptions to this are the fortresses of the Teutonic order to which an extra chapter has been devoted later on.

Nevertheless, certain factors may be associated with a regular type, for instance in the more western parts of Germany. Neu-Leiningen in the Palatinate, dating from around 1240, represents the classical line of the castle with four round turrets, even though the basic design is not so mathematically exact as, for example, in the Hohenstaufen castles in lower Italy. In the fortresses of the Rhine Valley also, a striving for regularity may be observed even in the buildings on mountain peaks. The Thurnburg (Maus) from about 1340, is such an example, with the watch tower on the outer side of the surrounding wall (ill. 156). Here flanking cover was not yet used, although towers for this purpose were already introduced in the 13th century in a number of fortresses, as well as in some city walls. Cologne is the chief example. Mainly in the 14th century, the military constructions of the Rhineland received their fully developed double gates, among which the Klever Tor in Xanten, begun in 1393, is the best preserved. In many cases, it is clear that new principles, particularly in the defence belts of the cities, were incorporated, from which can be inferred the dominance of the urban influence in the economic life of the time. Among others, Erkelenz is a beautiful example, where the fortress as well as the city wall has round flanking turrets.

The Rhineland castle usually has a vivid silhouette comprising buildings of varying height. The turrets were generally situated on the attacking front. The defence possibilities of the plain were increased by wall flanking. The Martinsburg at Mainz on the Rhine is just such a *randhausburg* with houses of varying breadth and height grouped around the courtyard (ill. 163, 164). This arrangement corresponds to a type which is widespread on the lower Rhine. The development there has quite a local flavour. The starting point is a roughly oval wall fortress, reminiscent of the motte plan (Hülchrath). After the success of the flanking principle the castle was further developed into a quadrangular castle, with corner turrets. This type was completely developed in the 14th century and may be seen at Gudenau, one of the most beautiful fortresses of the Rhineland (ill. 157). Gudenau's characteristic trait is a strong gate tower which forms a fortress in itself. Gudenau is thus a good representative of the gate tower fortress, a special form of the castle which is also found in northern Scandinavia. Moyland and Kempen are known for their well built round corner towers crowned by machicolation friezes. Gates with double turrets are also found in abundance (Haag, near Geldern). The development in Westphalia is closely related to that of the Rhineland. As a late example of that type, the castle of Assen may be mentioned (ill. 158). These valley fortresses, built in purely agricultural districts, had an exclusively defensive character. Their task was to protect the inhabitants against sudden attacks.

148 · *Schönberg near Oberwesel, Germany*

149 · *Eltz, Germany*

150 · *Eltz, Germany: dressing-room*

151 · *Marburg, Germany: Hall of the Knights in the castle*

152 · Marksburg, Germany

153 · Marburg, Germany: castle

154 · Coburg, Germany

155 · *Prunn, Germany: upper palace*

156 · *Thurnburg, Germany*

157 · Gudenau, Germany

158 · Assen, Germany

159 · Eltville, Germany: dwelling tower

160 · Pfalzgrafenstein, Germany

161 · Karlstein, Bohemia

162 · Otzberg, Germany

The connection of a main citadel to an advance citadel, with its domestic buildings, specially underlines this function. A close connection with the government of the surrounding countryside contributed to the fact that the valley fortresses, in the shape of feudal estates, grew into an organic part of the life of the age.

Like the castle, the turret fortress is particularly noteworthy in western Germany. Here there certainly appears to be a continuity between the Romanesque and Gothic periods.

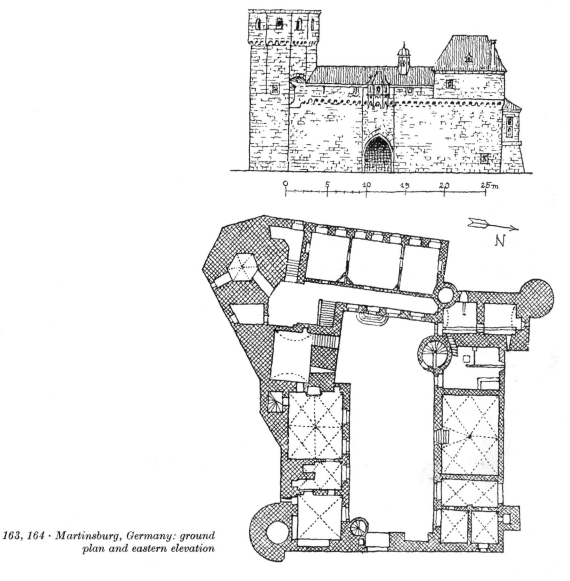

163, 164 · Martinsburg, Germany: ground plan and eastern elevation

Frequently the early residential tower has been incorporated in the structure of the late Middle Ages, as was the case in Eltz. A group in themselves were the fortresses built by the Archbishop Baldwin of Trier (1307—1354) during a feud. These are gathered around a main tower. Such a one is the mighty tower of Eltville, started in 1330 and joined to a castle (ill. 159). At Andernach in the electorate of Cologne the watch tower which has been partly adapted for residential purposes is adorned with Gothic decorations which were developed orginally on the main buildings and later transferred to the tower. An original construction from this group is the Pfalzgrafenstein near Caub, erected in 1325 on a small island in the middle of the Rhine in order to watch over the river traffic (ill. 160). The nucleus of this fortress is a tower surrounded by a wall in the shape of the bridge of a ship. At the same time, the whole presents a beautiful example of Gothic style.

During the Gothic period the well-tried tower fortress also appears on the Lower Rhine. Decorative details and hanging towers show connections with the rest of the Rhineland, and influences from France and the Netherlands are to be seen. The further development of the turret leads to solid domestic buildings from which it is only a short step to the more peaceful castles of modern times. Like every modified version of the tower fortress, there occurs in Lower Saxony throughout the whole Middle Ages, stone masonry which consists of a smaller turret-like building on the courtyard, where one's possessions could be put into safe keeping and where one could take refuge. It was similar to the earlier period when, as now, the tower would sometimes be quite large, rather like the Talwart Otzberg in the Odenwald, where the tower has grown into a large composite structure (ill. 162).

As the Eastern antithesis to this, we find developed tower-buildings in Bohemia, either standing alone or included in composite constructions (Wittinghausen, Kunzwarte, Raby near Strakonitz). In addition, in the years 1348—57, Karl IV erected a fortress in Bohemia in which Norman influence is even more prominent: Karlstein, southwest of Prague (ill. 161). The whole structure of the fortress is conditioned by physical features, and the outlines are dominated by two donjon-like residential towers, each of them containing a chapel, of which the St. Katherine chapel in the smaller tower has been well preserved and is famous for its beautiful architecture. The towers at Karlstein have rightly been compared with buildings such as Eltville on the Rhine which reminds us of the family connections of the Emperor Karl IV with Archbishop Baldwin of Trier. As regards the development of the residential tower in Bohemia in general, it may be assumed that the German Knights from Bavaria played an intermediary role here. In Bavaria, too, the tower fortress appears very early, just as in Austria and in Switzerland. The mighty Saldenburg, in the Bavarian Forest, illustrates the late development there.

AUSTRIA

Austria, being a stronghold of the Occident in the south-east, is unusually rich in citadels. Owing to the mountainous landscape there exists a bewildering variety of combinations of the old defence measures, walls, towers and fortified dwelling houses. This picture is dominated by a certain historic continuity from the very early days up to the threshold of modern times. In the eastern districts particularly, with their early Germanic settlements the castles develop in a direct line out of the constructions from prehistoric times, and the Turkish wars after the Middle Ages caused the castles to be further developed. This leads to the fact that it is often difficult to distinguish between a bastion and a castle. We can, therefore, only outline the main trends here. A more precise understanding of the geography of Austrian strongholds and the development of types can only be achieved by thorough

165 · Hardegg, Austria

166 · Viechtenstein, Austria

167 · Lebenberg, South Tyrol

168 · Landsee, Austria

169 · Neuhaus, South Tyrol

170 · Greifenstein, Austria

171 · Aggstein, Austria

172 · Heidenreichstein, Austria

173 · Rappottenstein, Austria: innermost courtyard

study of the subject which is at present being undertaken by the Fortification Research Commission in Vienna.

The tower as a timeless basic element in the architecture of citadels has played an important part in Austria, as has been briefly mentioned in connection with the Romanesque citadel. Here too, the classical period of castle-building began in the 12th century with the overlords and the church taking the initiative in the first instance, only to be superseded by Knights holding official positions and those nobles whose titles derived from the offices they held.

Meanwhile the permanent settlements on the arable plains and in the valleys had progressed sufficiently for the nobility to be able to go and live in the mountains, thus crowning the settlement with defence installations which, no doubt, had a psychological as well as a purely military end. The castle with its watch tower, being visible from afar, served to intimidate the enemy from a distance and to proclaim the might and splendour of the owner. More often that not, the tower was built first, as in the case of Steiermark. In Romanesque days the watch tower was purely a defence structure, and, with its slender appearance and square shape, it is reminiscent of the towers of Northern Italy. A larger building by the side of it served as living quarters and was rarely ornamented as artistically as were the palaces of the Hohenstaufen in Germany. These markedly utilitarian residential houses were connected with the watch tower by means of a surrounding wall, the extent of which was conditioned by the nature of the countryside. The harmony between nature and architecture is more clearly discernable here than elsewhere. The contours are predominantly practical with solid walls, even in cases where the structure has been fortified during the Turkish wars. Always, or nearly always, a Romanesque watch tower can be recognised as the nucleus of the fortification, for example in Viechtenstein in Upper Austria (ill. 166) and Hardegg in Lower Austria (ill. 165). Because of sound building technique the keep is often the only one still standing amidst the ruins.

Similar structures can be found in all parts of Austria, and the historical map of castles extends—in accordance with the old Habsburg sphere of influence—far beyond the present borders, beyond the wild mountain passes of the southern Tyrol, and Slovenia, as far as the Swiss territory in the west and Bohemia in the north. The *Burgenland* ("country of castles"), providing a series of advance posts, fully deserves its name. There Landsee (ill. 168) boasts a massive keep shaped like a enormous shell and facing the side from which attack was expected; in the course of time more and more defence belts were put round it. The stronghold, whose form is conditioned by the surrounding countryside, dates from the 12th century. It was later fortified as a border citadel, and in the 17th century bastions and casemates were added. In Forchtenstein, Lockenhaus and Schlaining, extensive additions were also made during the late Middle Ages and modern times. However, due to the peculiar character of the *Burgenland*, it was not always possible to take advantage of favourable landscape. The position was different in Styria (Dürnstein, Frauenburg) and Carinthia (Strassburg, Liebenfels), and particularly in the Tyrol with its numerous citadels which were thoroughly investigated by Joseph Weingartner. In that part of the country, irregularity to a high degree is the rule and here, too, the tower predominates (Neuhaus, Lebenberg-ill. 167, 169), except where natural conditions had made the erection superfluous (Greifenstein, ill. 170). These narrow, uncomfortable mountain nooks were not always inhabited. It has been proved several times that peaceful dwellings existed near the castle and only in case of danger did the inhabitants retire into the citadel. There are also watch towers which in form and position resemble Roman *burgus* castles although the central structure has grown higher (Hocheppaner chalk tower near Bolzano). We meet the same type of tower much later also in the shape of a strongpoint dominating the valley road, for instance near Finstermuenz, which was planned in 1471 as a toll barrier and constitutes the border between the Swiss Engadine and the Tyrolean Upper Inn Valley. A type by itself is the rock castle, which reminds one immediately of prehistoric retreats, which often sealed off an important mountain pass (Kronmetz in the Tyrol). This indicates a definite tendency to bar the most important roads by means of strongholds and towers although one should be careful not to have any exaggerated ideas about the system of strongholds in this connection. The Middle Ages thought in terms of short distances and, whenever defence measures were taken, purely private and immediate motives were as decisive as strategic ones. Often it was also an internal question of competing for power which led to the arrangement of one castle being built near the others, so that groups of castles come into being which could also do service within the framework of the country's defence.

The classical period of fortress architecture in Austria ends during the 13th century. In the case of those castles which were built in the prime building period, that is, during the last decades of the century, a certain change is noticeable. The most important factor is the growing emphasis on the residential quarters as compared with previous structures. The well known castle of Runkelstein in the Tyrol will serve as an example (ill. 174). It rises on a precipitous mountain with dwelling houses built close to the edge of the rock, thus reminiscent of the west German *randhausburg*. The foundations of the castles were laid in

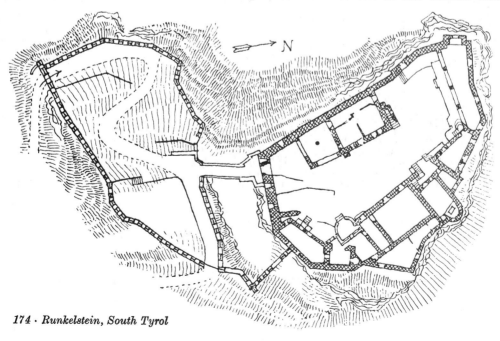

174 · Runkelstein, South Tyrol

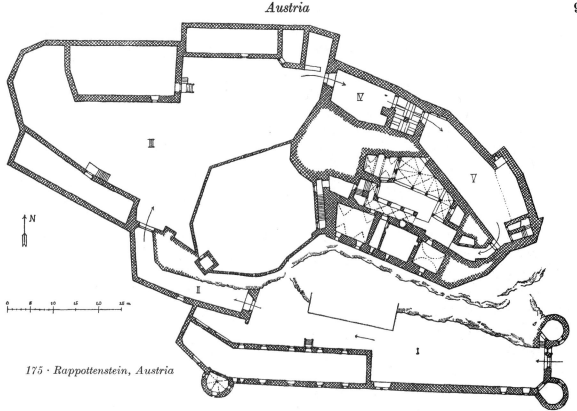

175 · Rappottenstein, Austria

the 13th century, and there have been many additions since then, on various occasions. The living rooms, with their numerous frescoes dating from the 14th century, and the impressive inner bailey, are world famous.

The 13th century also saw the watch towers beginning to be used as living accommodation. The new towers were more spacious and were given larger window openings as well as a more convenient division of rooms, although none of them achieved the form of the Anglo-Norman donjons (Brandis and Bruck in the Tyrol). Old towers, too, could be adapted and, along with habitable watch towers, residential towers were erected in which living accommodation is dominant (Krempelstein in Upper Austria).

The tower occurred even in the towns. Research has lately shown the existence of no less than thirty dwelling towers in Vienna and the same was true of St. Poelten and Krems by the Danube. They are reminiscent of Italian *casatorri* which may possibly have reached Austria by way of Southern Tyrol, where they were mentioned in contemporary writings.

Another change taking place simultaneously with the modification of the defence character of the main towers was the erection of outworks, the size of which was dictated by the landscape. People would entrench themselves behind fortifications consisting either of only the barbican entrance or of the weakest flank of the keep walls of the castle. Only rarely would walls be laid around the whole structure. At the same time, the outworks of the castle make a first appearance; this, in the early Middle Ages, had been unusual as special storage-rooms had been used. Now the castle developed into a large, independent unit, containing everything necessary within its walls. These structures have retained their great importance, particularly with regard to the social and economic life of the country, right up to modern times. The Lord of the Manor's household had the means of creating larger enterprises which the individual lacked. A good example of spacious layout is Aggstein near the Danube (ill. 171), a castle which, with its elongated design, is typical of that part of the country. The large outworks are fairly common in Upper and Lower Austria. Rappottenstein huddles like a miniature town around a Romanesque watch tower (ill. 69). After 1378 the citadel had considerable extensions added, and in 1548 even more decisive rebuilding turned most of it into a Renaissance castle (ill. 173, 175). In conjunction with the outworks, corner towers were used, which up to then had been hardly known in Austria. Heidenreichstein in Lower Austria has such semi-circular towers dating from the 15th century (ill. 172).

Although the general character of the castles during the later Middle Ages becomes more varied than during the Romanesque period, the general impression of most of the constructions is still one of practicability and compactness. The castles of the Rhine seem picturesque and gentle in outline as compared with those of Austria. That may be partly due to the softening influence of the South; also no doubt, the poverty of the country and the battles between East and West have contributed to the harsher appearance of the Austrian castles. Even where these buildings were mainly family residences they still had the function, far more than the Gothic castles of central Germany, of protecting the inhabitants of the country from the constantly threatening attacks. It is to be presumed, therefore, that the ancient functions of the tribal stronghold continued throughout the Middle Ages. At least this is what might be gathered from an index of the castles of Lower Austria dating from 1580 which contains particulars about refuges during the Turkish war. Conditions in ancient times are said to have been similar. It seems representative of the spirit not so much of attack as of defence, just as in the case of the ramparts of earlier days and the fortified churches of Transylvania. No doubt the Austrian castle has inherited its surrounding wall defences from the ramparts, this wall having been joined to the tower very early on. Even more direct is the connection with the traditions of late Antiquity where the development of the stone castle is concerned, more so than in the case of donjons and keeps in the Norman sphere of influence. The slender, fortified Austrian watch towers with their rectangular shape

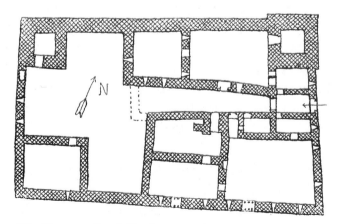

176 · Boymont, South Tyrol

seem to have the same origin in Byzantine structures as have the residential towers and slender castle towers of Northern Italy. It is quite feasible that further connecting links might be unearthed by more detailed research. In this connection a strange structure in Southern Tyrol might be mentioned, i. e. the Leuchtenburg. The main part of the building resembles a Shell Keep and probably has connections with the enlarged *burgi* of the Mediterranean countries. It is possible that the walls here, as happened so often in England, were a development of the old ramparts.

Of the development of the square fort the Austrian castle-complex does not tell us much, though even here the strict rectangular shape is not entirely unknown. Ebereau in the *Burgenland* is such a structure, dating from the 14th century but altered later. The most remarkable castle is Boymont which has the particular merit of a distinguished architectural style and an emphasis on residential comfort (ill. 176). The older parts date from the 13th century and are built in the style of the late Romanesque period. Judged only by its plan Boymont might be classed as a so-called 'water castle' but it does in fact rest partly on a level building site on a rocky summit. The fact that regularity may also be suited to higher ground is demonstrated even better by the northern part of the castle of Dürnstein by the Danube. It is true that many of the structures which are conditioned by their surrounding landscape give an impression of separate, unconnected clusters of castles but it is quite possible that a wider analysis which takes into consideration the social and economic factors, might easily discover a method in the apparent confusion.

SWITZERLAND

The Swiss castles show the influence of their three important neighbours, Germany, Italy and France, and although as regards castles the country is one of the richest in Western Europe a typically Swiss style of castle architecture cannot be said to exist. Apart from that there is much variation for this is the cross-roads of East and West. Quite frequently the structures are closely interwoven with the unusual natural surroundings. In Switzerland, too, the tower is the foremost feature, especially so during the early phases of stronghold building. This is shown in the case of the above-mentioned Habsburg family seat (ill. 178) which is only one example of many, where the tower is either the most important part of the structure throughout the Middle Ages or where it serves as the keep within a large castle composed of many parts. By studying those castles where the tower predominates, it is often possible to follow the gradual development of castles in general: how they break away from the settlements and the farming communities of the plains and move to the mountain peaks, symbolizing the new overlord status and safeguarding the economical and political interests of the settlement. In many cases this trend was abandoned half way through, which is evident from the existence of several village towers (Frauenberg).

However in most cases the move to the heights was a fortunate one and the result was a structure rising from the mountain peak or flush with the steep rock, which often perfectly caught the Gothic spirit with its serrated and flexible outlines, similar to the soaring towers of the cathedral. One example is Ortenstein, in the Grisons, with its inner tower dating from the 13th century and the other buildings which have been added successively during the course of generations (ill. 179). Then there is Rhaezuens on the left bank of the southern most head stream of the Rhine, a structure whose oldest parts date from the early Middle Ages (ill. 182). The castle was enriched by two inner towers which have since disappeared and which were connected by a surrounding wall and outbuildings. Rhaezuens is adapted to the landscape to the last degree and one can sense a groping attempt to copy nature, although its lines are quieter and more controlled. Depending on the type of building plot the castles were either conical or sectional with several variants. Today there are innumerable ruins which have become one with their surroundings, particularly in wild mountain country, now often covered with green woods. It was different when the castles were still in use. Then the mountain slopes had to be bare so that possible enemy movements could be observed. Often the windows offered a view across the valley, with its settlement spread out below like a map, a reminder of the roots where the castle had originated and on which its life depended. This is a development which, as regards the Grisons canton, has been particularly well described by Poeschel, who also explained the growth of the various types there, where the exchange with the other German-speaking countries was most pronounced.

In Switzerland it is not possible to draw a sharp dividing line between the purely defensive watch tower and the residential tower. The former is often more or less adapted for residential purposes whilst the residential towers retain sufficient defence installations to be ranked as military buildings. So it had been with the Habsburg and such is the case with the best-known tower structures like Thun (Berne canton) which was founded in about 1200 and had little corner towers added during the late Middle Ages. This is therefore closer to the donjons and keeps although its domestic character is not as pronounced as it is there. The simple tower was assured a place particularly in the State strongholds. The same is true of several feudal castles dependent on the Habsburg fortress of Kyburg (Hettlingen, Hegi) as well as Wildegg, one of the best preserved of the Argovian castles. From those and similar small castles the militant castle gained for themselves a powerful position during the later Middle Ages, being despised by the population who saw in the castle symbols of tyranny—a subject which was dramatized by Schiller. In most cases the residential parts of those castles were not of a particularly splendid character. Here as in ruling Austria usefulness and severity are the dominant factors. The main building generally contained storerooms, cellar and kitchen on the groundfloor (Rapperswil), sometimes even a stable. Such a main building could also assume the role of tower; it could either be the crowning glory of a mountain peak or be placed in a grotto where the mountain replaced part of the architecture and where only the facade had to be built. Kropfenstein is a good example of such a rock castle (ill. 180) which popular imagination is apt to connect with robber knights. Although during the Middle Ages usurpation was a perfectly legal procedure and although robbery was prevalent during the decline of the knightly orders it is not necessary to present the rock castle as being exclusively a robber knight's hideout. After all, the castles had various functions within their territory and one of them was to guard the most important mountain passes and roads which would

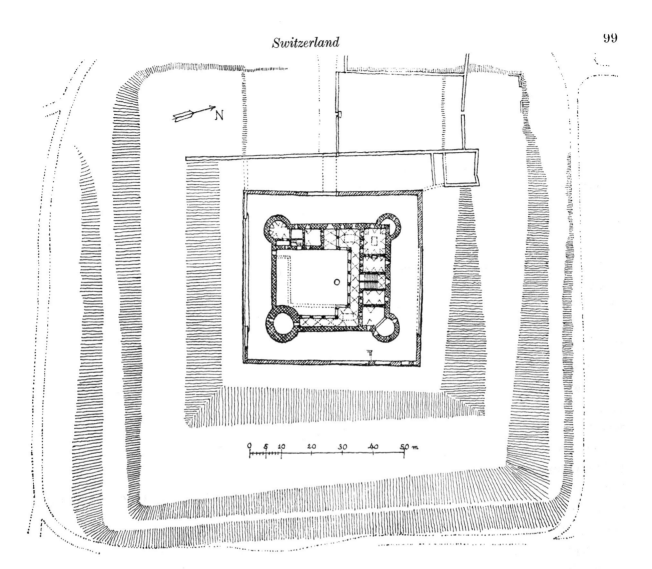

177 · Marschlins, Switzerland

yield revenue through toll charges and to control the traffic. It should always be borne in
mind that the castle was built with the idea of serving the owner's private interests even
if it granted asylum to the serfs and the workers, who were the economic basis of its
existence.

Chillon by the lake of Geneva is one of the largest, best preserved castles in Switzerland
and is a good illustration of the fact that a division into mountain and water castles
cannot be a wholly satisfactory (ill. 181). The ground plan and grouping of Chillon's various
buildings is typical of castles safe on the top of a mountain, although in this case the most
important defence installations are the lake and a strong fleet of ships. The oldest parts are
the inner enclosing walls and the lower section of a strong keep from Romanesque days.
During the 13th century the surrounding wall was strengthened and succesive epochs have
busily contributed to give the castle its well known outlines with machicolation friezes
ornamenting tower and walls. Several defence elements point to the influence of France,
which is easy to explain, for Chillon had belonged since about 1150 to the Count of Savoy,

first as a feudal tenure and later as his property until 1536. The interior is famous for its 13th and 14th century frescoes on walls and ceilings of most of the rooms. Byron (1816) and Victor Hugo (1839) have assured Chillon a place in world literature.

For good reasons rectangular forts are not numerous in Switzerland. However, there are a few examples of which Marschlins in the Grisons canton is the most remarkable (ill. 177, 183). The castle is built strictly symmetrically with three semi-circular towers and one complete round tower at the corners. The flanks have been completely rebuilt, and the interior contains nothing from the Middle Ages. Marschlins was begun during the second half of the 13th century and from its ground plan one can hazard a guess at a certain similarity with the strongholds that Frederick II erected in Southern Italy. Perhaps this is where Marschlins got its inspiration: the castle belonged to the territory of the Bishopric of Chur where most bishops were ardent followers of the Emperor. A closely related type of castle is found in the Vaud canton and can be explained by the influence of the House of Savoy. Thus Aigle is a stronghold of masonry with three round corner towers and one strong main tower (ill. 185). The buildings within the courtyard are not connected with the actual surrounding wall. Aigle only acquired its present appearance during the restoration by the Bernese who conquered the castle and village in 1475. Champvent dating from the 13th century, also in the Vaud canton, belongs to the same category.

A later development is represented by Vufflens (ill. 184), built between 1395 and 1420 by Heinrich von Colombier, a vassal of Amadeus VIII of Savoy. The castle consists of a mighty watch tower, surrounded by four low, square corner towers, and connected with the rectangular residential building, which is flanked by four corner towers, by means of walls. Here, however, greater emphasis was placed on the domestic functions. The architecture was influenced by Northern Italy.

During the late Middle Ages several older structures were enlarged. The castles built on mountain peaks rarely had outworks added because there the best use had already been made of the countryside. But so far as possible the castles were given 'keep' walls which can be best observed on the flat ground for example at Hallwil (Aargau) which was first built during the 11th century on a small island to seal off the important roadway to the Rhine. The original Romanesque building, a solid residential tower, was later fortified by the addition of outworks and surrounding walls with projecting towers. Quite a number of towns, too, were given surrounding walls with flanking towers during the later Middle Ages (Freiburg, Murten) which testify to the power of the towns through the growing importance of currency dealings. This last development was also one of the factors which eventually caused the collapse of all feudal power.

THE LOW COUNTRIES

In the Middle Ages the division of the Low Countries into several small counties, fights with the powerful neighbours in the south and west and internal strife provided good reasons for defence architecture, and many examples survive today in Holland and Belgium despite the extensive destruction that took place there. As in Switzerland, building was partly

178 · Habsburg, Switzerland

179 · *Ortenstein, Switzerland*

180 · *Kropfenstein, Switzerland*

181 · Chillon, Switzerland

182 · Rhäzüns, Switzerland

183 · Marschlins, Switzerland

184 · *Vufflens, Switzerland*

185 · *Aigle, Switzerland*

influenced by the neighbouring countries, France and Germany. But quite early a strong local strain is noticeable and an endemic development begins, particularly in Holland.

The Burcht at Leyden is one of Holland's oldest and certainly most remarkable castles (ill. 189). It consists of a surrounding wall of round design placed on a hill. There is also a shell tower, although the walls do not reach the same height as is usual in England. Leyden rather resembles the motte structures with its circular wall replacing a palisade. This wall has a gallery supported by arches, which later became a characteristic of the defence architecture of Holland and the Lower Rhine. Leyden dates from not earlier than 1150 and is therefore the first example of such a construction. The ground plan, too, points to the future.

Because of the flat countryside the ring-fort is a favourite type in Holland and Leyden was soon imitated at Teylingen and Oostvoorne. Whereas Leyden was used exclusively as a retreat and had no buildings within its precincts, a main building was added somewhat later to Teylingen and a central tower to Oostvoorne (ill. 186).

Such a design might have been appropriate as long as the defence was only horizontally and vertically arranged, but it was quite unsuited to any flanking movement. One could make do with towers added at a later date as has been done in Oostvorne and other ring-forts

186 · Oostvoorne, Holland: reconstruction

like Kessel and Wouw, but this was not really satisfactory. A combination of the old keep with a polygonal stone wall was not an ideal solution. In the 13th century therefore, the ring-fort makes room for a rectangular design, thus introducing the square fort into Holland's architecture. The best known example of this kind is Muiden (ill. 187, 190). Round flanking towers were added to the corners of this strictly symmetrical structure. From the northern side of the courtyard rises a hall which was built when the castle was started in 1280 under Floris V. This castle, however, was destroyed after its owner was murdered round about 1300 and was rebuilt on the old foundations during the second half of the 14th century, when a residential wing was added on the eastern side. In this form Muiden represents a typical *randhausburg* of the kind also to be found in the German region of the Lower Rhine. There are several other examples like Brederode, Medemblick (1288), Amersooien (about 1300, later reconstructed ill. 191) and, above all, Helmond which dates from the early 15th century and is now used as a town hall (ill. 193). These castles show a clear affinity with the French strongholds and their round towers, though with a local appearance. That the contact with France was a very real one is proved by, amongst others, one building which is now destroyed. That building is Sluis which was planned by a French architect in 1384.

Besides the square fort the turreted castle has played an important part throughout the whole of the Middle Ages in Holland's defence architecture. The oldest specimens go back to Romanesque times and are no longer in existence. But the latest excavations—particularly those under J. Renaud—show clearly how they followed close on the old motte tradition as had been the case in Oostvorne. When, in the 13th century, the aristocracy began building in earnest it was the kind of tower that fast become a typical feature of the countryside, that is, not the purely military structure, but the fortified house which guarded the owner and his household against enemy attacks. This group developed a style peculiar

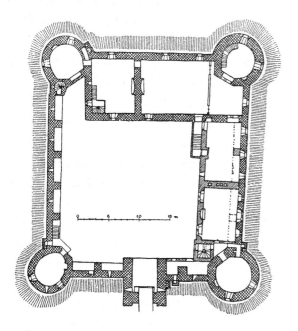
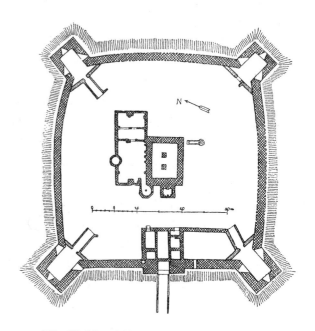

187 · Muiden, Holland   *188 · Wedde, Holland*

to Holland as regards design and manner of building, using brick cleverly in the construction and ornamentation. Not many specimens have survived but a number of beautiful buildings still exist, most of them having been reconstructed later. The tower is nearly always the starting point. As a rule a wing is built on to this nucleus of the structure thus creating an L-shaped ground plan. The corners of it were interconnected by a surrounding wall, thus forming a small inner courtyard. Doornenburg from the 14th century is such a feudal seat, typical in its cubical shape of Dutch defence structure (ill. 192). Joined on to the main part of the castle were the outer works with the domestic outbuildings; this, too, is characteristic of agrarian Holland during the late Middle Ages. On the other hand, the outer works could equally well be grouped around the keep as was the case with the fortress of Wedde which illustrates the development of the Dutch castle through the centuries (ill. 188). First the traditional tower was built, possibly during the middle of the 14th century, and in accordance with custom it was situated on a hill. In the 1470's, while the civil war was raging, the palisade around the tower was replaced by a surrounding wall which was in turn replaced by a new one after the Middle Ages. At this time—about 1530—a hall was joined to the old tower. However, the demand for domestic comfort grew, and the outline became more graceful as in the case of the fortress of Croy at Stiphout (North Brabant), where the building almost completely lost its defensive character (ill. 194). These structures were occasionally and quite naturally adapted to modern conditions when firearms were invented. There are several examples of how cannon towers were introduced into older existing castles (Horn, Stein).

In Belgium today the castles have much in common with the Dutch, although in most cases the French influence predominates. The most outstanding defensive structure in Flanders is the Gravensteen at Ghent (ill. 195), residence of the Counts of Flanders, which was built in the 1180s by Phillipp vom Elsass in place of an older castle. A broad donjon in the centre, reminiscent rather of the English hall-keeps after the manner of London and Colchester, dominates the whole. But in comparison with the English counterparts the Ghent donjon is more severe in style, its outer walls being divided by simple pilasters, and inside there is only one large room on each floor amongst which the Great Hall is justly renowned as one of the most interesting and characteristic interior rooms of Romanesque castle architecture. The purpose of this donjon was merely defensive and representative. Many important events in the history of Flanders have taken place in the Great Hall and our imagination should fill the Banqueting Hall with such scenes as are illustrated in *Les Très Riches Heures du Duc de Berry*. A main building was already built in Romanesque days to serve residential needs on the West side of the donjon with a communicating passage leading to the state rooms in the tower. These buildings were ringed by an oval-shaped wall which in its ground plan is reminiscent of the Dutch ring-fort. The outside of the wall has many buttressess built in. When the flanking principle became more common the wall was supplemented in a peculiar manner: a suspended tower was fixed to every other buttress in the French manner which gave better protection to the castle but also a strange appearance. There is nothing like the Gravensteen to be found either in Belgium or in any other country, although the turreted fortress was to occupy an important position in the castle architecture of Flanders (Laarne, Brustem, Terheyde).

Subsequent building in Flanders tends towards the composite structure in order to satisfy the demands of defence as well as comfort. The polygon with flanking towers at the corners which had grown out of the ring-fort was a favourite in Flanders and kept its position until the end of the Middle Ages, after which time it was modernized (Gaasbeck Castle) or completely rebuilt. A brilliant survey of these now demolished structures is contained in *Flandria Illustrata* (1644) by Sanderus even though the illustrations are much simplified. From this the important part which the castle played in Flanders can be reconstructed. Occasional examples have been preserved although in a changed form, amongst them Cleydael, a typical *randhausburg* with fluctuating outlines.

Vorselaar, restored in 1663, with its abundance of varied façades demonstrates the dissolution of the late medieval period and its adaptation to the more sophisticated life at Court (ill. 196). The details remind one partly of those castles which the late Middle Ages were so fond of setting up as ideals in the elegantly illustrated books of hours. Walzin shows the same tendency (ill. 198). This castle is built close to a precipitous mountain side and points its defence towards the more easily accessible side. The unassailable façade on the peak, on the other hand, has the air of a palace in a Burgundian town. The very opposite of Walzin is Beersel near Brussels (ill. 197), a ring-fort which in 1491 was fortified by the addition of strong flanking towers. Its appearance heralds the coming of the battery towers and the double gates of the tower which the towns installed during the last decades of the Middle Ages (Bruges, Mecheln). In the Flanders' towns it can be seen more clearly than elsewhere how the rich merchants not only took the initiative in the art of building fortifications but also gave the appearance of a castle to their public buildings. Town Halls and Cloth Halls (Loewen, Ypres) are decorated with pinnacles and little corner towers, and watch towers and bell towers, symbols of the up-and-coming bourgeoisie, are named after the famous *bergfried* (Bruges, Ghent). The castle has become a symbol of dignity, similar to the development in other West European countries.

CASTLES OF THE TEUTONIC KNIGHTS

In 1230 Herman Balk was the first marshal of the Teutonic Order to go east with his knights to start the conquest of the Kulmerland and the adjoining Prussian districts. This was a direct continuation of the crusades to the Holy Land and, due to the peculiar constitution of the Order, a new chapter in the history of citadel building in the Occident began. The Order originated in 1198 from a hospital fellowship which had taken over from the Hospitallers (the knights of the Order of Malta) the rules pertaining to nursing, and from the Knights Templar the military rules. The rules of the Order, therefore, combined the samaritan with the knightly which in architecture called for a union of monastery and castle, a programme which was carried out to the letter in Prussia, with the castles of the Order as its most dignified result. In addition the German-Baltic brick Gothic style

189 · Leiden, Holland: the Burcht

190 · Muiden, Holland

191 · Amersooien, Holland

192 · Doornenburg, Holland

193 · *Helmond, Holland*

194 · *Stiphout, Holland: Croy Castle*

195 · *Ghent, Belgium: Gravensteen*

196 · *Vorselaar, Belgium*

197 · Beersel, Belgium

198 · *Walzin, Belgium*

influenced these utilitarian buildings with its characteristic features and turned them into first-class works of art.

However, the early castles of the Order in Prussia are hardly conspicuous for their originality. Because it was essential to have operational bases immediately after transferring the Order to Prussia the first strongholds were built in places where the castles of the old inhabitants, the Pruzzes, had stood. In this way the new structures were adapted to a large extent to the older strongholds and were quite often built as sector castles. Even those citadels which were started in completely new places close to the most important highways did not, during the first 30 years, follow the square-fort principles. The Engelsburg is therefore still dependent on the surrounding landscape. Balga II (ill. 199) which was built towards the middle of the 13th century, although more symmetrical, cannot yet be classed as a typical castle of the Order; it could more aptly be compared with the conical castles of Western Europe. With Koenigsberg II (started in 1258) this first period comes to an end and a new era of building begins for the Order. The new type, which now emerges as successor to the castle blended into the terrain, is built in the shape of a long rectangle, a camp castle, as also survives later in the smaller fortresses. The early examples of this category show that the houses in the courtyard were made of wood and only after the suppression of the

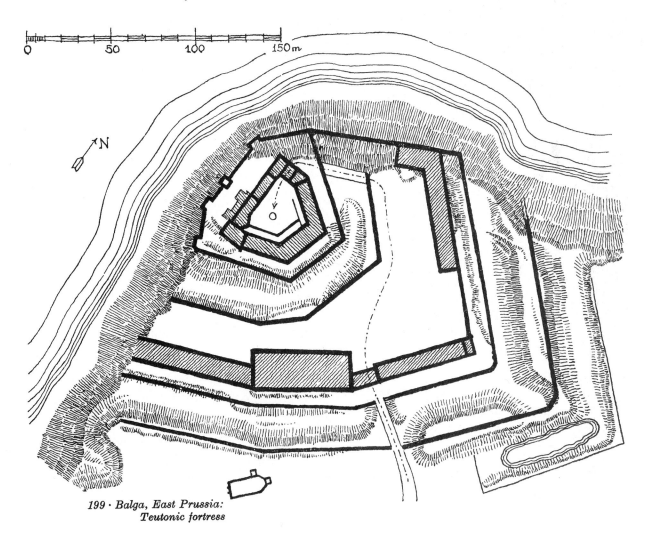

199 · Balga, East Prussia:
Teutonic fortress

200 · Rheden, West Prussia: reconstruction of the Teutonic fortress

rebellion in the 1260's was it possible to use stone to any large extent. In the 30 years between 1260 and 1290 the actual castles of the Order emerge and the camp castle which had been planned on a broad basis consisted, in the main, of dwellings concentrated on a so-called conventual house.

The conventual house—*domus conventuales*—can be traced direct to the social structure of the Order. As a rule the convent of the Order consisted of twelve friars who, led by the commander of the Order, formed a community subject to strict rules. For these reasons large assembly rooms like chapel, chapter, dormitory, and refectory were necessary. The most suitable method proved to be to house these rooms in four wings grouped around one courtyard, making the structure look like a cubical block formed by the welding of the four houses. Gradually the camp castle became an enclosed quadrangle. The most important rooms, chapel and chapter, were the first to be joined in one part of the house, a combination which has been maintained in all conventual houses. From the end of the 13th century onwards the conventual house is the leading type in the architecture of German Orders. In Lochstedt and Marienburg it is already developed during the late 1280s; later follow in quick succession Mewe (ill. 206) with its slender corner towers, and Rheden (ill. 200), with even greater integration of architectural style and late Gothic refinement of detail. At Rheden the old German watch tower is joined to the castle, as had been the case in Strasburg, where the main tower measuring 180 feet is still intact. The free standing watch tower of Schlochau near a corner of the castle is a tangible example of the gradual assimilation of a main tower. Where it faces the fields the four parts which go to make up the conventual houses are often marked by gables, providing the North German art of brick-building with an opportunity to display its liking for ornamentation. The courtyards were given arboured walks like the monasteries but in contrast to the seclusion of the monasteries there were several floors; the main rooms were on the upper floor, probably for reasons of safety. The flanking positions in nearly all conventual houses are rather conservative, with the possible exception of the fortress at Schwetz (1345) where the corners were given round towers, crowned by battlement friezes. From the beginning the Order displayed a particular liking for barbican structures.

The most distinguished memorial in Prussia was the residence of the High Master. The Marienburg makes possible a survey of the whole architecture of the Order from the end of the 13th century up to the catastrophe of Tannenberg in 1410 (ill. 201). The oldest part—the Hochschloss—consists of a conventual house to the south, a closed quadrangle around a courtyard the corners of which are given slender towers in the style of Mewe and Rheden. At first there was no East wing. In 1309 the High Master left Italy in order to make Marienburg his main seat. This was the beginning of a brilliant epoch in the history of the castle. The conventual house was completed, the chapter and the chapel in the North wing received their final shape and were decorated with elegant star vaults. The desire for larger, more representative rooms breaks through the compact block of the outer appearance; the chapel choir juts out of the mass of building in the East and is the exception to the rule in the development of conventual houses. The courtyard was ringed by cloister-like galleries which served as communications between the various wings. From the south-west corner of the Hochschloss a passage led to the cesspool tower or *Dansker*.

The outworks, too, were subsequently surrounded with buildings and given the name 'middle castle', whilst to the north a new set of outworks was constructed giving the castle the appearance of being divided into three, with a frontage of more than 550 yards along the river Nogat. The most remarkable part from the first half of the 14th century is the Master's Main Refectory (ill. 203), which, with the graceful lines of its vaulting, conveys a specially beautiful picture of the interior architecture of the Order. Light brick vaults stem like palms from the slender granite pillars, which are a recurring feature of the Order's art, the whole being a mystic creation with gentle light effects. For the vaulting with three-beamed ribbing, the Order received its inspiration from England. Soon, though, the foreign influences were incorporated into its own wealth of form and in the Teutonic brick-producing countries the star-shaped vaulting received its specific character which was to leave its mark during the Middle Ages and even beyond in all countries around the Baltic. Lovely examples of this are contained in the West wing, the last important stage in the building of the Marienburg, a highlight of the Order's architecture. The West wing was the actual residence of the High Master and therefore equipped with princely splendour. The lofty summer refectory, where one single pillar supports the rich vaulting, was much admired (ill. 202). It was while he was under the spell of this room that Eichendorff spoke of architecture as 'music turned to stone'. Whereas the outer façades of the old high castles were severely compact with only monumental stone-faced niches and narrow arched friezes or generously spaced diamond-frets of glazed stone in the expanse of wall, the appearance of the West wing is far removed from such an ascetic attitude. Level with the Refectory windows the pilasters are replaced by twin pillars of granite; the grand decorative construction of the defence passage in particular contains elements pointing to French influence which might have penetrated via the Rhineland and the Low Countries. The façade looking out over the courtyard is similarly openly constructed. Inside, the same two-dimensional structure of the wall gives to the passage outside the summer Refectory a light, diaphanous appearance that is unequalled among the secular building of the Middle Ages. The groups of buildings constituting the West wing is reminiscent of its counterparts La Roma and La Miranda in the 14th century, and also of the papal palace at Avignon.

As a further unique symbol of the soldierly religious ideals of the Order there stands in the niche of the East window by the chapel choir a statue with inlay of the Madonna, 26 feet high, facing East, and designed to be seen from afar like so much at the Marienburg. It was destroyed in 1945.

The bishops' palaces in the Teutonic countries were directly influenced by these mighty patterns. Here, too, the conventual house became predominant; after all the convention of the Order usually served as model for the dean and chapter, and several members of the chapter had to belong simultaneously to the Order. These circumstances are confirmed at Marienwerder, one of the most distinguished bishop's palaces in Prussia, dating from the first half of the 14th century (ill. 204). The exterior of Marienwerder is dominated by the massive cess-pool tower, the most magnificent in all Prussia. In Heilsberg we encounter another beautiful example of episcopal architecture. The main castle is designed to serve as conventual house with a well balanced courtyard surrounded by arcades, which gives a lighter impression than those of the castles of the Order (ill. 205). The origin of the Teutonic castle has long been a favourite subject for discussion with research-workers and the main question concerns generally the influences from the Orient and Mediterranean countries. The greatest expert on castles of the Prussian Order, Karl Heinz Clasen, has come to the conclusion that the true Teutonic castle developed more or less independently. He denies the existence of direct influences from the Holy Land and Southern Italy. It remains a fact, though, that there is a certain connection between the conventual house and the Southern castles and that it occupies a special position in North European architecture. The purely external circumstances mentioned above may have been the reason why the conventual house was not the main type from the start. However, the ideal of the square-fort type was already there which is evident from the attempt at symmetrical outlines in the early castles which conformed to the terrain. When the country was finally subjugated and building in stone became general, the plans were drawn up

201 · *Marienburg, West Prussia: Teutonic fortress*

202 · Marienburg,
West Prussia: Summer Refectory of the Teutonic fortress

203 · Marienburg, West Prussia: Great Refectory of the Teutonic fortress

204 · *Marienwerder, West Prussia: Bishop's palace*

205 · Heilsberg, East Prussia: courtyard of the Bishop's palace

206 · Mewe, West Prussia:
Teutonic fortress

207 · Arensburg, Saaremaa Is., Estonia: Bishop's palace

208 · Reval, Estonia: town wall

209 · Narva, Estonia: Hermannsburg and Ivangorod

partly taking into consideration local physical conditions. Whereas in the South the surrounding wall constituted the main part of the castle, in the Teutonic countries it consisted of four wings which, in contrast to the narrow square castles of Italy and the Orient, are characterised by a clearcut design. Instead of the uniformly built mass of the South the North accentuated its style with gables on the corners. In that respect the Teutonic castle is closely related to the square castle of the Rhineland, and the Order has indeed adopted much from that direction. However, in the Rhineland and the Low Countries the whole group consists of houses of differing width and height, whereas in the Teutonic countries a severe style, reminiscent of the South, with wings of equal height on each side, predominates.

In 1237 the Teutonic Order succeeded the Order of the Sword in the Baltic countries. More than a hundred years later (1346) the Danes sold their provinces in Northern Estonia to the Knights of the Teutonic Order who were to rule the land from Samogitien to the Finnish Gulf and from the Baltic to the Peipus Lake. The Order, however, were by no means the only ones with this ambition. The Church also owned much real estate, the vassals made a third ruling power in the country, and the Hanseatic towns a fourth. All these groups lived in constant feud and they also had to be constantly on their guard against their Russian neighbours, for their relationship with the oppressed inhabitants of that country was anything but friendly. These circumstances contributed to a tremendous boom in defensive building, the largest in the history of the Baltic North. Leading the building of castles was the Teutonic Order with its wide experience gained in the Holy Land, Hungary and Prussia. But the development in the Baltic countries, the *Terra Mariae*, did not progress as logically as it had done in Prussia, the *Terra Petri*. The Baltic countries had used stone for their buildings even before the advent of the Order and had been in contact with Scandinavia, the Rhineland and Westphalia. In contrast to the brick-producing Prussia, there was plently of limestone in western and northern Estonia, and in the Dwina basin in Southern Livonia. In other parts of the Baltic countries the use of boulders was preferred. As in Prussia, the Order preferred to build its first castles on the sites of the old fortresses of the original inhabitants, which influenced the later buildings. Watch tower and surrounding wall were of the type that was emerging in the Rhineland, Thuringia and Hesse. From the end of the 13th century, however, the conventual house was introduced, took the lead, and by the 14th century was firmly established in that position. There are several examples to be found, either reconstructed (Riga, Windau) or in ruins (Wenden). During the second half of the 14th century, the Order founded a mighty structure at Reval on the site of the old Estonian-Danish castle which incorporates features from the Rhineland in its defence system, particularly in the main tower called Langer Hermann (ill. 208). At the same time similar work was begun on the Hermannsburg at Narva, the most easterly fortification of the Teutonic Order in northern Estonia (ill. 209). The original Danish plan was considerably enlarged: a mighty tower was added—here, too, called Langer Hermann—to the north-west corner and a building rather like a cess-pool tower was joined on. In 1944 the Hermannsburg was still well preserved in odd contrast to the

210 · Narva, Estonia: reconstruction of Ivangorod

essentially different Russian border fort, Ivangorod, which faces it on the other side of the river Narva (ill. 210).

Just as in Prussia, in the Baltic countries, too, the larger episcopal castles are built like conventual houses. Hapsal in north-west Estonia dates from the 13th century and shows in its oldest parts connections with the artistic development in the Rhineland and Westphalia. Arensburg on the Oesel (ill. 207), the best-preserved medieval castle in the whole of the Baltic province, was built in the 14th century as a conventual house. The dolomite which is found there made possible different forms from those found in Prussia, not only in the interior but also as regards the outward appearance. In contrast to the brick buildings of Prussia with their many ornaments, Arensburg has heavier art designs in cut stone and seems to be descended directly from the Cistercian (Benedictine) style of monastery rooms. This difference is noticeable in many Baltic castles and helps towards an even greater appreciation of the art with which flat surfaces were treated in Prussian buildings.

SCANDINAVIA AND FINLAND

The Scandinavian North reflects the new tendencies in defensive architecture of the 13th century although the material used is much poorer than that of the old battleground between East and West, the Baltic countries and Prussia. The hitherto predominating tower as centre of defence is being gradually displaced by larger composite structures. King and Church continue to lead in the architecture of castles, the buildings of the aristocracy being as a rule fortified houses without any visible aggressive character.

In Sweden, considerable changes in the development of the castle were caused by the rule of the Imperial Administrator Birger Jarl (castles in Stockholm, Nykoeping and Oerebro, now completely rebuilt or destroyed). The wall becomes increasingly a connecting link between the various parts of the castle, much more so than in the past when tower and main buildings were independent structures within the surrounding wall. Neither tower nor main buildings, though, attain the dimensions reached in Central and Southern Europe; the

211 · Sverresborg, Norway: reconstruction

Nordic castle remains largely utilitarian and a change was to occur only during the final phase of the Middle Ages. Up to the middle of the 13th century the flanking system had not gained a foot-hold.

The position in Denmark was similar. The picturesque castle ruin of Hammershus, on the rugged northern cliffs of the island of Bornholm, contains masonry from several periods (ill. 213). The oldest part consists of a massive square residential tower, the lower part

212 · Kalmar, Sweden: reconstruction

of which probably dates from the middle of 13th century. A square inner courtyard is joined to the tower, with houses along the surrounding wall. The entrance being in the main tower, Hammershus belong to the gate tower castles. The brick bridge, across the outer moat, is remarkably well preserved.

Conservatism is evident also in Norway, a country whose geographical and historical circumstances make it unsuited to the building of large-scale castles. From time immemorial the Norwegians were known to prefer fighting their enemies on the water and the royal castles were for preference built along the coast or near other waterways. One of the oldest of them was Sverresborg near Trondheim (ill. 211), where, as at Hammershus, the main defence was centred on the gate-tower. Akershus in Oslo was a composite structure on a larger scale with a strong central tower. Ragnhildsholm, now belonging to Sweden, was built during the 13th century as a Norwegian border fort and is composed of a rectangular building with a strong projecting square tower, which is rather reminiscent of Gutenfels on the Rhine. The first perfect manifestation of the flanking system to be found in the Scandinavian North is on the town wall round Visby on the island of Gotland (ill. 214). This mighty building from the second half of the 13th century, which is the equal of the greatest previously mentioned examples of its kind, was probably modelled on those of the Rhineland, most likely the town wall of Cologne, whose Severin Gate is to be found in a simplified form on the Visby wall. The many sacred buildings on Gotland dating from the 13th and 14th centuries also provide evidence of the undoubted connection with Rhineland-Westphalia. The building of the long wall around Visby which measures nearly two miles took some considerable time and provided a living for a large number of masons, who were much in demand, after their work was finished, as builders of fortifications in the Baltic countries. The older parts of the town wall of Reval speak for themselves—a group of master builders from Visby worked there before the wall, with its strong semi-circular towers, was completed in the 15th century (ill. 208). The masons from Visby surely left their mark also on Åbo in Finland where the castle, begun towards the end of the 13th century is like a camp castle in miniature with two mighty towers and a surrounding wall. The castle was later extended in several phases but achieved its present size only after the Middle Ages. The largest building enterprise after the wall of Visby in southern Sweden is the royal castle of Kalmar, which was begun towards the end of the 13th century. Originally, the castle consisted of an irregular four-sided circular wall with a slightly curved east frontage (ill. 212, 215), a round tower on each corner and two square gate towers, each of which represents a castle in itself after the pattern of the Rhineland gate tower castles (e. g. Gudenau). The towers of Kalmar are the first Scandinavian round towers in the French manner which had come via the Rhineland. For many decades Kalmar remained the exception in Northern architecture. Only in the second half of the 14th century was the flanking of the round tower seriously considered and then particularly in Denmark under King Waldemar IV (1340—1375). The great wall round Vordingborg, with its semi-circular flanking towers of brick, was built during his reign. Similar features may be found in Kalundborg, and in Norway, where Tunsbergshus stands, the most complete structure with flanking

213 · Hammershus,
Bornholm Is., Denmark

214 · Visby, Gotland Is., Sweden: town wall

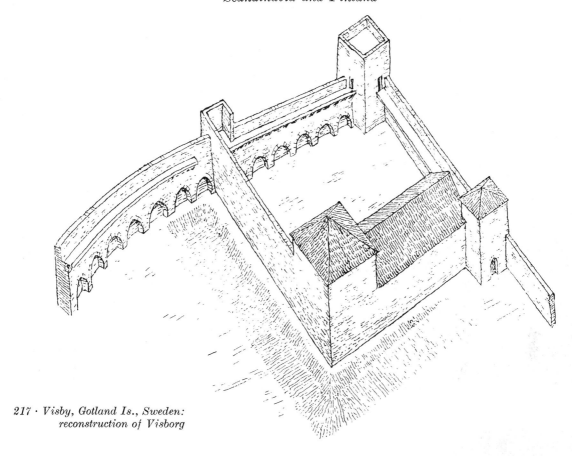

217 · *Visby, Gotland Is., Sweden:*
reconstruction of Visborg

towers in the whole of that country. This series of surrounding walls with round towers attached follows closely on the development in northern Germany and the Baltic countries (Schwetz in West Prussia with its round towers from the middle of the 14th century and the 'Langer Hermann' at Reval from about 1370) all of which are in turn based on the models of the Rhineland and Westphalia.

Simultaneously with these castles and town walls, with their fully developed flanking towers, there exists another style which can only be described as conservative. Castles like Tavastehus in Finland and Vaestervik in Sweden, now destroyed, form a severely closed square with rectangular corner towers without any flanking characteristic. These castles reflect clearly the influence of the Teutonic Order which was in its prime at the beginning of the 15th century in the reign of King Erik. As early as 1407 the Teutonic Order had planned a castle on Gotland which was built by Erik in 1411. This is Visborg, at the south-west corner of the famous wall round Visby; only parts are still standing (ill. 217). The model in this case, though, was not the conventual house, prevalent during the 14th century, but the camp castle which developed alongside with the conventual house in the countries of the Order. The connections with the territory of the Teutonic Order are even more evident in the castle of Krogen on Oere Sound, which was begun in 1423. In its place there stands today Hamlet's castle of Kronborg but research has revealed that portions of Erik's structure, partly restored were incorporated. The Great Hall with its fan-vaulting closely resembles the Refectory of a Teutonic castle but here the square courtyard is no longer completely surrounded with houses, just as in the case of the old Malmoehus which was also started by Erik. The relations between Erik of Pomerania and the Teutonic Order, though not always friendly, played an important part in his policies. One of the first champions of a *Dominium maris Baltici*, Erik attempted to regain Northern Estonia for Scandinavia. He had an opportunity of enlarging his knowledge of the internal affairs of the Teutonic countries when he concluded a treaty with the High Master in 1423 whom he met in Neustettin. It is significant that the foundations of Krogen were laid immediately following that meeting. The ancestral castle of Ruegenwalde in Pomerania is another proof that ideas received from the Order were being incorporated. This is where the exiled king fled, taking with him a legendary fortune in art treasures, after holding out obstinately for ten years in his fort Visborg.

During the second half of the Middle Ages the turreted castle does not lose its importance altogether in the Scandinavian North, but it begins to play a different part in the 13th century. The system of central defence had lost its former importance and this caused the tower to be developed increasingly as an independent structure suitable for residential purposes. Now and again, though, the tower retains its original purpose, particularly in cases where it stands on the site of an older castle like Korsoer in Denmark where Gurre

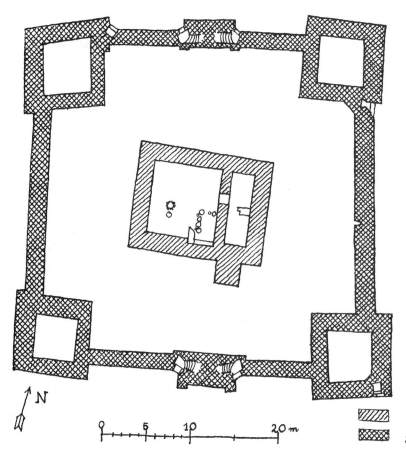

218 · *Gurre, Denmark*

also was a characteristic building (ill. 218). The foundations of the central tower seem to date back to a late Romanesque structure but in the 14th century Gurre was extended under Waldemar Atterdag and given a surrounding wall with strong corner towers. This wall occupies an exceptional position in the architecture of Danish castles and the model is probably to be found abroad, either in the Teutonic countries or the Mediterranean. A unique example of the development of the turreted castle in the North is the main tower in Haelsingborg, on the Swedish side of the Oere Sound, which was probably built by Waldemar Atterdag in the 14th century as a royal castle. The tower was the king's residence and stood, a symbol of might in the old manner, where the river joins the Baltic, and in sharp contrast to the camp castle opposite, Krogen in Helsingoer, the old operational base of King Erik. Once again the tower dares to show itself rising proudly in Gjorslev on Zeeland, seat of the Bishop of Roskild, Peder Jensen Lodehats. It is designed like a cross with a strong central tower, rather like Trim in Ireland and Rushen on the Isle of Man.

During the final phase of the Middle Ages the single-structure castle grows in importance, particularly in the internal development of Denmark and Sweden. The builders were the country's aristocracy and old traditions often reappear in the designs. The changes in fighting techniques leave hardly any mark on these castles; they cling to the idea of passive defence and rely mainly on thick walls and isolated rooms. A surprisingly good example of such fortified houses survives in Glimmingehus in southern Sweden Scania, Danish until 1658, (ill. 216), built in 1499 by Adam von Dueren, a masterbuilder from the Lower Rhine who did much work in Denmark and Sweden towards the end of the Middle Ages. But even later the fortified house was much favoured as seat of the lord of the manor.

CASTLE—FORTRESS—PALACE

THE INTRODUCTION OF FIREARMS

From 1370 onwards firearms begin to play an increasingly important part. In 1378 the castle of St. Angelo in Rome was bombarded; Tannenberg in Hesse was completely demolished in 1399 with the aid of the new weapons. By the beginning of the 15th century the artillery had become so effective that the taking of counter measures could no longer be avoided although these did not, to begin with, revolutionize all the old principles of defence. This did not happen until the second half of the 15th century, and the victory over the Turks at Rhodos in 1480 was an event of far-reaching importance. The effectiveness of cannon fire had been thoroughly tried out—for a long time to come fortified walls and the thunder of cannons were to form an inseparable pair of the horrors of war.

The effect of firearms wrought a complete change in all defence principles hitherto in use. The medieval castle had concentrated on the defence of the elevated parts, and a decision was forced by the hand-to-hand fighting. The aggressor either directed his attack against the foot of the wall in order to undermine it, or he tried to reach the top of the wall in order to gain entry into the defence passage and thus reach the interior of the castle. In both cases it was advantageous for the defender to occupy as high a position as possible in relation to the attacker. Catapults and crossbows did not become effective until the second half of the Middle Ages, which led to the perfection of the tower system.

In the early stages the cannons did not differ vastly from the elementary catapults of the same period for they, too, had to be stationed near their target because of their short range. In the beginning psychological intimidation was the strongest weapon, causing walls to be constructed more massively than was necessary. But the new weapon was soon to be improved, and as a result changes in the way of life of the social levels followed one another in quick succession. The leading and most compelling principle in the construction of defence building was that of neutralizing or destroying the effect of the striking power of the new weapons. The age-old method of defending heights lost its importance, the towers grew lower and thicker. As the cannon, rampart gun and arquebus were further improved, the effective distance between attacker and defender diminished and led to the building of more sprawling outworks. Guarding the flanks now became even more important than it had been in the Gothic castles, while adaptation to the landscape became almost meaningless. The ideal design was a mathematically simple lay-out with low cannon or martello towers between rectilinear wall sections which either take the shapes of star, triangle, polygon or other geometrical figures, or retain the old fortress design. Solid earth mounds come to the forefront.

The revolutionary influence of firearms on social circumstances was as great as their technical significance. The age of the knight was finally past. The first blow had been delivered by the cross bow because the knight, heavily armoured for single combat, was usually helpless and clumsy when confronted with crossbow. The knight's individualistic attitude towards battle was gradually being replaced by the striking power of the masses, a course of events furthered by the use of the arquebus which for a long time was used simultaneously with the crossbow.

And what changes were wrought in the life within the old, distinguished castles! The strains of a gay life with music, dancing and worship of women had long since died. Cultural life had moved to the towns, knights existed in name only and often enough this was connected with atrocities and robbery. According to Ulrich von Hutten only the uncouth voices of the hired soldiers could now be heard in the castles and there was a foul stench of gunpowder and dogs. Of course, there were still exceptions but the arrangement of combining defence and residence could no longer be maintained. The medieval castle had reached its prime through the union of these two elements and its history ends with their divorce. The result is that the palace as we know it grew out of one branch and the ever stronger fort out of the other. The building of defences could hardly now be left to private enterprise but was the concern of kings, sovereigns and towns, who alone could afford them. These buildings entailing enormous earthworks, were often abandoned half way through when funds dried up. Defensive architecture by this time had quite lost all private characteristics. History had come a full circle, arriving at the same point as that prior to the conversion of the collective fort, the ramparts, into a feudal castle.

ITALY—FRANCE—ENGLAND

The introduction of firearms did not come as a surprise to the fortress architecture of Italy, France and England. Here, where in 1195 outside Dieppe, Greek fire brought back from the crusades had been used, strong round towers had been built since the 13th century which stood up well to the new weapons. For once defence had outstripped offense. The massive round towers of Lucera, Aigues-Mortes and Coucy differ only in detail—for example, in the embrasures—from the new cannon towers in their early stage of development. In Italy the new system grew organically out of the round tower and the old preference for clear-cut regular lay-outs. A structure like the 14th century Sarzanello, north of Pisa, shows in its balanced triangular shape the way forward (ill. 219). Castel Nuovo at Naples was started in 1279—1283 by the House of Anjou but was finally completed as late as 1442. The thick, low, round towers with loophole friezes in the battlements date from that time. A castle of similar design is Rocca Pia at Tivoli (ill. 225), built by Pope Pius II in 1460. Old traditions there have been retained but the defensive character is more dominant than before and the building gives the impression of a fortress rather than a castle. Now and again an attempt was made to unite the new defence system with castle-like buildings. A famous structure of that kind is the Sforza castle at Milan, which was rebuilt in a new shape in 1450. Large court yards dominate, the defence is concentrated in massive, low round towers and imposing gate structures, where the defence details unite into one artistic whole. Although the medieval character lingers on in this architecture, the decorative element is already stronger and the total impression is festive and inviting. The spirit of the renaissance had taken a firm hold on the old building habits.

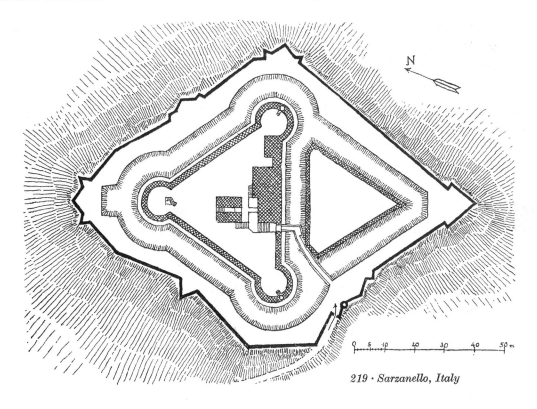

219 · Sarzanello, Italy

220 · Greil, France: reconstruction

From the second half of the 15th century the castle in Italy tends to sever itself more and more from the pure fortress, the former growing into the artistic renaissance palaces of the towns, the latter standing dark and threatening for hundreds of years with enough strength to defy the artillery fire. Because of surprise attacks by the Turks it was most important to fortify the coastlines. The old Hohenstaufen fortress of Manfredonia, for example, was given a tower and walls of a new design in 1458. The defence structures in Gallipoli by the Gulf of Taranto are also impressive with their round low defence walls that might almost be called bastions. In order to strengthen the resistance of the towers the outside of the walls were sloped, until finally the bastions, early in the 16th century, began to take over the role of the tower.

From now on the castle builders are no longer anonymous. Francesco di Giorgio is the first of a line of distinguished renaissance artists to occupy themselves with defensive building. The bastions and gates designed by Michele Sanmicheli in Verona in 1520 were models of construction. Lastly, Leonardo's designs for heavy cannon towers with bomb-proof casemates should be mentioned.

In France a presentiment existed as early as the 14th century of the tendencies to come. When the building of the Bastille in Paris was begun in 1369 the towers were still placed in the traditional positions. But when, after many years' work, the fortress was finished, new principles of defence had to be considered: the towers were kept lower, on a level with the partition-walls with which they are linked, and gradually the castle was turned into a compact fortification. The castle at Tarascon (about 1400) belongs to the same category although there the attempt was still made to unite fortress and residence. Gothic residential buildings of the castle type can be found in Josselin (Brittany), a beautiful early example of the transition from fortress to castle (ill. 227).

In the case of small structures like manor houses, the cannon towers were put directly on the corners of the main building with the effect of uniting defensive and residential purposes in the manner of the Middle Ages. The fact that comfort was not forgotten in the interior of castles is evident from the larger windows and balconies. Apart from this detour, the development about 1500 led to the famous French castles where medieval defence details became largely decorative, whilst the style of the renaissance gained a strong foothold in the interior. This is the explanation for the castle of Greil (ill. 220) where the Gothic verticalism and delight in ornamentation have a last fling. The abundance of towers is not motivated

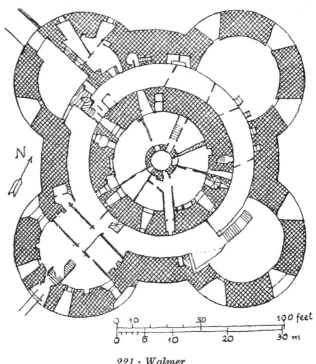

221 · Walmer

by any thought of defence; the old defence structures are simply used in playful decoration. It is to this time that the romantic period of the previous century went to find its Gothic, and the novel *Nouvelle Heloise* by Rousseau used this scenery in imagination.

As in Italy, a second development led logically to the actual defence structure. A perfect example was the castle of Ham, which was a victim of the first World War. Furthermore, a number of older fortifications were equipped with ordinance towers (Arques, Dijon, Langres). Town walls were supplemented with gatehouses that could stand up to firearms (Flavigny). A specifically modern type of defensive building did not, however, emerge and was hardly necessary: the power of Louis XI had become almost absolute after the suppression of the obstinate Provençal feudal lords. France was on the threshold of her great epoch and her wars were waged outside her boundaries.

But even the free Baroque-style castle, the Louvre included, did not quite manage to shake off one remnant from the old fortresses—the moat. A narrow bridge is built across it towards the stately main portal, the latter giving a certain aloofness.

At about the same time as in Italy and France, castle and fortress in England also parted company. Towards the end of the 15th century, much of the strength of the castle was sacrificed for comfort. An example of this is Hurstmonceux, where the architecture of the tower goes back to Plantagenet traditions, but, as in France, is very ornamental. The great days of castle building had left their mark on English thought, so that even in the castle of the Renaissance and the late Gothic period the tower and battlements were retained as symbols of dignity. Walpole's *Gothic Story* and Langley's building theories make use of this medieval repertoire, thus providing later professors of architecture with material for their lectures.

As regards the technique of fortifications, firearms caused as little surprise in England as in Italy and France. One has only to remember the solidity of the Plantagenet tower. Of course, much had to be altered, the embrasures had to be adapted for arquebus and culverin and made their appearance towards the end of the 14th century although the modernisation had not then been completed. One of the earliest examples is the gate-house at Cooling, finished in 1380. The new type of fortress was not complete until much later, during the reign of Henry VIII (1509—47), when the break with Rome and the general tension in England's internal and foreign politics made defence measures along the south coast necessary. Accordingly a number of modern forts were built around 1540, e. g., Walmer (ill. 221), Deal in Kent, Camber in Sussex, St. Mawes (ill. 226) and Pendennis in Cornwall. Partly modelled on Italian fortresses, these buildings were constructed in the shape of compact concentric blocks, with a strong, low bastion in the centre, surrounded by semi-circular cannon platforms, casemates and ramparts. The precision, the emphasis on usefulness and the careful execution of these castles of Henry VIII mark a very definite step forward towards the defence architecture of modern times.

GERMANY—AUSTRIA—HUNGARY

The introduction of firearms made its largest impact in *Germany* where massive flanking towers were rare and where most of the towers were insignificant in size, or indeed in many cases were missing altogether. The perfection of firearms led to solid round wall towers being built all over Germany. Here, too, this development causes the severing of residential from defensive purposes although these two elements remain linked for a longer period of transition than was the case in Italy and England.

The first task was the extension of older structures, often conditioned by the surrounding country, which often led to a compromise between old and new. The first example which springs to mind is Prozelten on Main, a Romanesque castle which, from 1320 to 1483, had

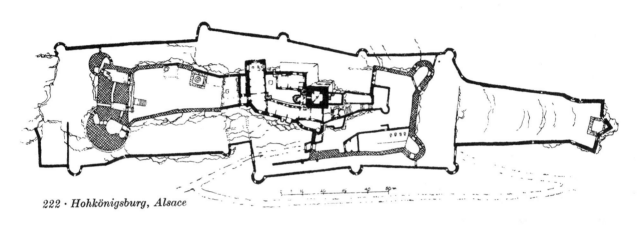

222 · Hohkönigsburg, Alsace

belonged to the Teutonic Order. The Order had adopted the new fighting methods comparatively early and altered its architecture accordingly. At the beginning of the 15th century Prozelten, too, was provided with a defence wall with closely spaced towers, which were still fairly slender, which had been adapted for the lighter firearms. A considerable structure which was extended in the German manner is Hohkönigsburg in Alsace (ill. 222) where, as at Prozelten, the central part dates from the Romanesque period and managed to survive the destruction of 1462. In 1479—1481 the castle was adapted to the demands of the times and amongst other additions was given a mighty tower linked with a thick barrier wall, successor of the old sentry wall. Despite the mixture of old and new elements the Hohkönigsburg was well able to withstand artillery fire until it partly collapsed under the fire of Swedish cannons in 1633. An appearance of particular strength is conveyed by the castle of Hartenburg in the Palatinate (ill. 223), to which cannon towers were added during the last decades of the Middle Ages. Here too the basic principles of the sectional castle have been preserved, the sentry wall being replaced by a massive projecting bastion that defends the vulnerable side like a clenched fist. The interior contains strong, bomb-proof rooms. Büdingen in Hesse, with its Jerusalem gate dating from 1502, had new low towers of strange artistic formation, sporting oddly shaped helmets above the purely decorative tracery friezes of the battlements. Advance forts of different types belong to this group, particularly strengthened gates like those at Cologne and Goerlitz. The most

223 · Hartenburg, Germany

striking and best preserved building of that type is to be found in Poland, however—the
Barbakane of Cracow, started about 1500 (ill. 228).

With the advent of firearms the old castles steadily lost their importance, built as they
had been with a view to the defence possibilities of the surrounding countryside, and seldom
were cannon towers added. Those castles, on the other hand, which were built on the plain
in the midst of closely populated agricultural districts, retained their role in the defence
of the country. In this category are most of the castles of the Lower Rhine and Westphalia.
There the main influence had been French and Dutch, which attached great importance to
the flanking principle and the round tower. There the new look largely meant the retention
and continuation of tradition. Residential and defensive structures were combined in different
ways. In the case of smaller structures the cannon tower was usually placed at the corner

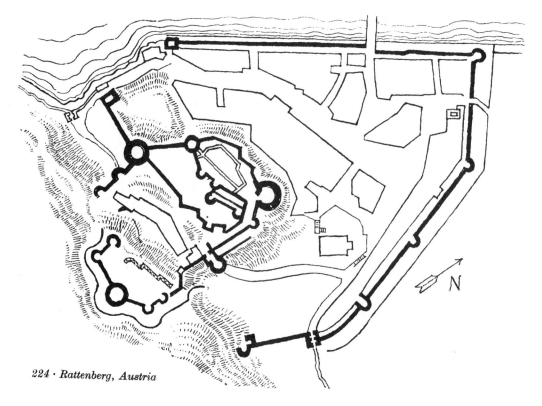

224 · Rattenberg, Austria

225 · Rocca Pia, Italy

226 · St Mawes, Cornwall

227 · Josselin, France

228 · *Cracow, Poland: barbican*

229 · *Kufstein, Austria*

230 · Salzburg, Austria: Archbishop's palace of Hohensalzburg

231 · *Salzburg, Austria: Great Hall of Hohensalzburg*

232 · *Nagyvázsony, Hungary*

233 · Nedec, Poland

234 · Smederevo, Jugoslavia

235 · Golubac, Jugoslavia

236 · Constantinople: Rumeli Hissar

237 · *Bauska, Latvia: Teutonic fortress*

238 · *Olofsborg, Finland*

of the residential building, more or less as it had been during previous centuries (e. g. Sandfort, Assen in Westphalia, ill. 158). In this respect the Gothic, Renaissance and even the Baroque style combine here. In the case of larger and stronger fortified buildings the defence belt and residential quarters were divided by putting a rectangular wall round the castle proper with round towers or low corner bastions. A lovely example of this style is the castle of Hardenberg near Neviges. In other districts, too, cannon towers are to be found which have been added to castles from the late Middle Ages or the Renaissance, as, for example at Friedewald and Wolkersdorf in Hesse. So far the old master builder tradition from the Middle Ages still predominated in all these buildings. Here Albrecht Dürer was inspired to write his treatise (1527) on the fortification of towns, castles and boroughs, which contributed considerably to the propagation of the new defence method.

The best specimens of the emancipated German castle are to be found in the towns. The basic type might be considered to be a square ground plan with residential wings round an inner courtyard with corner towers, although variations do occur. Here, as in France, the towers were given a more decorative appearance. So far the partitioning of space and architecture of courtyards had not arrived at the clarity and simplicity of the Southern European Renaissance, and in some parts the picturesque grouping of the Gothic style still prevails (the castles at Stuttgart and Dresden, as well as Hartenfels in Torgau and Gluecksburg near Flensburg).

Due to Austria's role as bulwark between East and West, the advent of firearms caused much building activity. The first to be tackled were the main fortresses which, in the interests of national defence during the 15th and 16th century, had solid extensions added, such as connon bastions, barrier walls and casemates. From 1530 onwards Ottenstein in Lower Austria was turned into a modern fort with symmetrically spaced round towers and bastions. In the Tyrol (ill. 229) Kufstein, Sigmundskron and Rattenberg (ill. 224) stand out as the mightiest structures of the time. All these examples are extensions to existing castles which had to be adapted to the irregularities of the originals, although the basic ideal was the mathematically calculated fort. Rattenberg with its newly constructed bulwark and a strong bastion in the centre actually followed the ideal pattern. An exception is the famous Hochosterwitz in Carinthia which was given its present form in 1570—1586. However, on the apex of this colossal conical mountain there had already been a fortress which has almost completely vanished today. The new structures abound in defensive detail, gates, draw bridges, pinnacles, embrasures and bastions. The whole is an impressive testimony to the country's determination to defend itself during the critical 16th century.

The attempt to weld old and new into one organic unit often succeeded, the result being a fortified exterior and a castle-like interior. The inclination of the late Middle Ages to construct rectangular courtyards made it easy for the 16th century to add loggias in the Italian manner (Rappottenstein, ill. 173). An idea of the medieval courtyard can be gained in the Tyrol (Gojen and Fürstenberg). Proesels in the Eisack valley has a well preserved late Gothic loggia with ornamental frescos. The delightful courtyard of Churberg (Vintschgau), with its intentionally pseudo-archaic marble pillars, testifies to the way in which the late Gothic blended effortlessly with the Renaissance. The archbishop's fortress of Hohensalzburg is the most dignified example of the interior decorations of the late Middle Ages (ill. 230, 231). This structure also shows the stages of development in castle architecture from the Middle Ages right up to modern times. The nucleus of the castle rests partly on Romanesque foundations. Considerable alterations were undertaken under the Archbishop Leonhard von Keutschach (1495—1519), providing this lofty building with such beautiful rooms as the Great Hall and the Golden Room with their fine wainscoting. In contrast to these playful decorations stand the clumsy battery towers. Further examples of the high standard of interior comfort during the late Middle Ages can be found in Reifenstein and Fuerstenberg in Vintschgau, Tyrol.

Hungary had always had to reckon with attacks from the East, and its largest fortresses had always been planned with a view to defending that border. Castle architecture received a new impetus after the Tartar invasion of 1241, when Bela IV called on a large number of German and Italian builders in order to build castles. At the same time he advised the aristocracy to follow his example. Many a tower castle bears testimony to this activity (Sárospatak, Nagyvázsony, ill. 232). The tempo of building increased in the 14th century when Hungary grew to a leading position under Ludwig the Great (1342—1382). A considerable number of ruins from those days show how in the stirring times of the 15th and 16th century similar reinforcements were undertaken as were usual in Austrian and German defence building. First of all strong round towers were added, as, for example, at Nedec (now Polish), a structure from the 14th century which had originated as an important barrier gate on the road into Poland (ill. 233); at Sebes, with its mighty sloping round towers from the 15th century; and in Trencsén, one of the most important and oldest fortresses which had successfully withstood the onslaught of the Tartars. Amongst the castle-like structures

239 · Vajdahunyad, Hungary

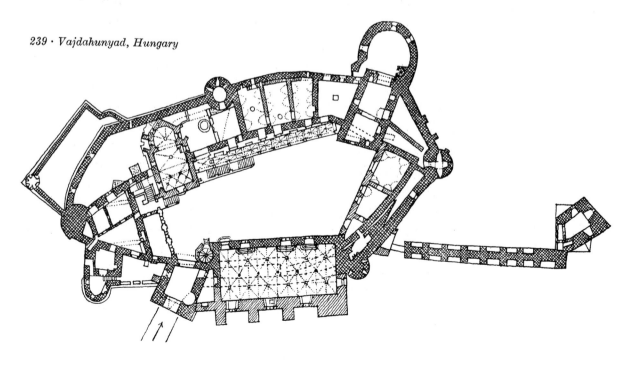

Vajdahunyad occupies an exceptional position (ill. 239), and is one of the few Hungarian castles still standing, thanks to extensive restoration work during the 19th century. The main front is dominated by a huge palace, in the façade of which Italian traits can be recognised, but adapted in such a way as to show a certain kinship with Avignon and the Marienburg. Vajdahunyad's most important parts date from about 1430; the defensive belt was later made complete by the addition of round towers and bastions in the Italian manner.

WEST AGAINST EAST IN THE BALKANS

The struggle in the Balkans between the Slav and central European civilisations, between East and West, between the old Greek-Byzantine heritage and the influence from the North, leaves its mark on the defence architecture. The heterogeneous nature of the country become evident especially towards the end of the Middle Ages, a dramatic phase where in the most far-reaching event is the conquest of Constantinople by the Turks in 1453, a catastrophe which was preceded by lively activity in the building of fortifications.

Many of these structures have their roots in Antiquity, for instance Argos in Greece, a comprehensive fortification on the Mount Larissa with partly pre-historic foundations (ill. 240). Argos is not actually a castle in the usual sense but a citadel which resembles the European town walls. In the architecture of the tower French influence by way of the Franconian feudal lords in the 13th century can be seen. In 1388 Argos was attacked by the Venetians; in 1483 it was taken by the Turks who added to the defence belt. This course of events is typical of the Balkans.

The chief carriers of Western achievements during the late Middle Ages were the Venetians who built quite a number of castles about 1420 along the Dalmatian coast and the Levant, which were of an entirely martial character. The traditions of the pre-Turkish era are still evident in the castles of Jugoslavia today; they are based on a completely different type of layout from that of central European castles, owing to the peculiar social conditions of that country during the Middle Ages. These buildings have a certain resemblance to country castles but Byzantine fortresses and south Italian castles have also contributed an influence. In Serbia there is the monumental surrounding wall of Smederevo on the Danube. With its closely spaced, square flanking towers it demonstrates how the old Byzantine traditions persisted even in 1430 (ill. 234), the same period during which the Balkans were busy preparing for the threatening attack. The building technique, with intermittently inserted lines and patterns of small bricks, is directly reminiscent of the Constantine era, and only the ecclesiastical Slav inscriptions and a Greek cross, rising menacingly to warn the enemy, tell us when these buildings were erected. A chain of castles like Kupinik, Rudnik and Zemum, with their rectangular design and round or square towers, give the impression of desert fortresses of ancient times. Elsewhere clumsy towers of either square or conical shape predominate; Golubać, with its wall towers which cling to the rocks rising from the Danube, is the most telling example (ill. 235).

Similar buildings often furnish the basis of Turkish building activity. To begin with they, too, incorporated the Arab traditions of ancient times with their strong towers and wall

240 · Argos, Greece

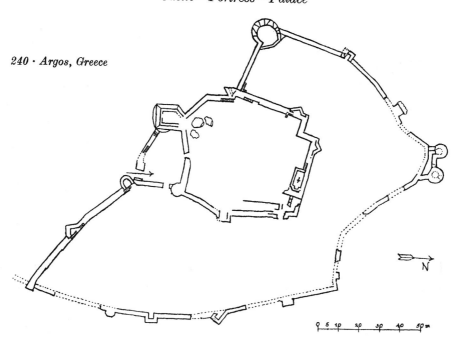

defences which gradually they tried to adapt to firearms and which had served them well outside Constantinople. In Ruomeli Hissar, on the shores of the Bosphorus (ill. 236), built between 1454 and 1456, making use of two existing older towers, the traits of the Turkish citadel and border fortress emerge clearly. In Yedi Coulis, built in 1458 to reinforce the Golden Gate at Constantinople, the design was star-shaped and this points to a development which became a leading feature some time later in Italy. But mostly the Turks held fast to their own traditions, and the walls and towers for a long time to come use the basic principles of the Greek designers. This stage might be called the closing phase of medieval defence architecture which was to become most popular in Russia and of which the most outstanding example is the circular wall of the Moscow Kremlin dating from the years 1480—1490. However, as will be shown, similar developments occured even further north, again caused by the struggle between East and West.

SCANDINAVIA AND FINLAND

It has already been pointed out that the Teutonic Order was one of the first in Northern Europe to adopt the new fighting methods. The first castle to be designed with a view to firearms was Buetow in Pomerania which was completed shortly before the battle of Tannenberg in 1410. With this castle a completely new element enters the architecture of the Order. The structure consists of a rectangular surrounding wall with a square tower at one corner and round towers at the three others which were already designed for defence by arquebus. On one side of the courtyard is the main building which, however, no longer dominates the whole front as had been usual in Teutonic castles. Meanwhile the social structure within the Teutonic Order had undergone a change; the hired soldier succeeded the knight and the imposing assembly rooms had therefore become superfluous.

In 1410 at Tannenberg the combined Lithuanian and Polish forces defeated the army of the Order, whose commander-in-chief, High Master Ulrich von Jungingen, was killed. This defeat had a profound effect on the strength of this Prussian Order and the castles it was able to build. After 1410 only negligible extensions were added to the castle, of which the round towers of the Marienburg are the most noteworthy. The power of the Bishops was more successful in continuing any building activity. Admittedly, no new structures were extended in accordance with the new defence demands nor from an artistic point of view (e. g. Heilsberg, Allenstein and Roessel). It was the renegade towns who took over the lead in architecture from the Order, a state of affairs which has a parallel in the brick-producing districts of Northern Germany. The magnificent gate-towers at Anklam, Demmin, Luebeck, Neubrandenburg, Pyritz and Stendal spring to mind, where in many cases, they were placed outside the older defence walls. Defensive purpose and civic pride are here blended artistically with a delight in decorations, lace-pattened ornaments are set on crystal-clear outlines, in stark contrast to the softly picturesque garlanded walls of the West (Rothenburg on the Tauber, Dinkelsbuehl).

The effect of the introduction of firearms on castle architecture is much more pronounced in the Baltic countries than in Prussia. Internal feuds between different groups tended to encourage the construction of strong defences. This and the growing pressure from the East caused tremendous efforts to be made, particularly from the 15th century onwards. Some of the older castles were reinforced with cannon towers and quite a number of new structures were added, for instance Bauske which was built in 1443, at the southern border of the Order country. Two round towers are placed at the entrance, one of which is the largest in the Baltic countries (ill. 237). Of the castles at the eastern border, Neuhausen, in the bishopric of Dorpat, is especially imposing and one of the cannon towers on its east side had a niche built in the shape of a Latin cross as a border landmark against Russia. In the reign of the Order's Master Wolter von Plettenberg (1494—1535) many older castles were reconstructed and modernised, as a last attempt to protect the Teutonic countries from the Russian menace. This building work was particularly extensive in the residence of the Order's Master at Wenden. The best known of the castles which were brought up to date at that time is Riga, where the old 14th century castle was extended by the addition of diagonally placed cannon towers. The building was finished in 1515 and in this modernised form it has influenced many other castles in the eastern provinces.

Meanwhile, the Russians were not idle—East stood against West here rather as it did in the Balkans. If the Episcopal castle at Neuhausen had a Latin cross facing east, Isborsk, on the Russian side, only a few miles away, had thick cannon towers built with a Slavonic cross facing west. The counterpart of the Hermannsburg of the Teutonic Order at Narva was the sprawling Russian border fortress Ivangorod on the east bank of the river, which was begun in the 15th century and later extended (ill. 209, 210). Among the leading masterbuilders was a Greek, Marcus de Grece, whose influence is felt in the architecture. Ivangorod is clearly an off-shoot of those camp castles and border fortresses which developed in the Balkans from ancient traditions and which were later taken up by the Turks and the Russians.

By way of Russia the Greek type of castle also reached Finland, as Olofsborg shows (ill. 238). Sixteen foreign masterbuilders were at work there in 1477 and the design as well as the conical towers, later made higher, clearly show the builders' country of origin. Like the hired soldier, the military builder could sell his services to the other side if he thought it more profitable. Olofsborg is an exception in late medieval defence architecture and the Scandinavian North has no equivalent either. The time around 1400 does not constitute a dividing line between architectural types. It is likely that there had been lighter firearms early in the 15th century whose range, however, was not sufficient to cause any considerable change in castle architecture. Compared with the development in Central Europe a certain conservatism is evident in the feudal castles of the days of King Erik. During the middle and second half of the 15th century few castles were built, which may be due firstly to the existence of internal unrest which influenced building by the Crown and secondly to a decree forbidding the private builder to erect fortified houses. Only towards the end of the 15th century is there any increased activity on the part of the Crown, the Bishops and the aristocracy, but even then no immediate adaptation to the demands of the new weapons is noticeable. In its defences the castle of 1500 is distinguished by its conservatism: towers are generally non-existent, which is in sharp contrast to the development on the Continent. Only the beginning of the 16th century saw new trends in Scandinavia also: the round tower, adapted to firearms, is introduced. Even so, the development is not general; at first, only the royal castles, and later the Bishops' castles, adopted the new style as, for example, the Archbishop's Palace of Steinvikholm near Trondheim in Norway dating from about 1520, where the diagonally placed corner towers are modelled on those at Riga. During the second quarter of the 16th century, a number of feudal castles in Scania adopted the same design (Trolleholm, Torup, Vittskoevle), and it is probable that builders from the Baltic countries did some of the work. These structures represent the Indian Summer of the Teutonic Order's architecture; here the truly medieval habit of combined defence and residential purpose is still maintained. The same is true of Gripsholm, the ancestral castle of the Swedish king, Gustav Wasa, which was begun in 1537 under the supervision of Henrik von Coellen who had emigrated from Prussia. This construction, which in its obstinately individual form, was to become the scene of so many historic events and which means so much to Swedish national feeling, was to be Scandinavia's last castle in the medieval sense of the word. The numerous castles erected later in Sweden by Gustav Wasa and in Denmark by Christian III were more and more divorced from defence and the established patterns of life in North Germany and the Low Countries.

Conclusion

Under the compulsion of the rapid improvements in firearms in the 16th century, the fortification buildings had to be kept lower, and the parts between the buildings had to be transformed and reinforced. In most cases, the towns were the initiators of the new defence situation, and it was chiefly there that the modernisation was carried out. Almost all countries contributed to the improvement of the defence measures and the new ideas were more widely spread than ever before. Defence begins to become international. The invention of printing contributed to spread new ideas and many pamphlets on defence buildings and theories concerning them were published.

All the new buildings incorporated the principles contained in the pamphlets, though the medieval masterbuilders' traditions were still in use. The new system lays more emphasis on the outworks in order to shift the defence front forwards as far as possible from the castle building itself, and therefore it slowly loses its old functions. This striving for innovation was expressed in the ramparts and bastions, an independent section in front of the main fortification. Here also, a return of the original style is to be found from the ramparts, through the assault walls, to the fortification of the new era. The town archives of Braun, Hogenberg and Merian give some idea of the gigantic effort needed in the construction of the huge fortifications of the 16th and 17th centuries. The engineers enthusiastically used different theoretical systems and calculations, and from then onwards the bastions and ramparts were constructed like the ornamental parts on baroque furniture. In order to connect practice with the reality of war, the town buildings and the castles seem to disappear more and more behind ramparts which, except as an impressive sight, were of no use. Only the entrances are emphasized in a special way, and much could be said about these baroque gates in a separate chapter. The four gates of the main entrance at Danzig are among the most vivid examples, allowing one to wander through several centuries of gate architecture. Often, important masters of the baroque such as Fischer von Erlach, Tessin and Vauban were devoted to defence constructions which do not seem to show any connections with the older type castles, except the heavy machicolation tower of Balthasar Neumann, on the south slope of the Marienfeste, at Würzburg, which is included in the old defence system.

What is now to be the destiny of the medieval stronghold under the pressure of the new defence system? The development went on quite logically, and just as the knight retired from the scene under the pressure of the new circumstances, so the stronghold as a defence system was defeated for the same reasons. However, for a long time, several strongholds could maintain their positions, owing to favourable situations, and to the help of bastions and rampart belts, but this occurred only rarely. We find, however, that the rapid improvement of firearms and the new pattern of warfare precludes any reliance on strongholds and castles as before, and the final decisive battles are waged in the open fields. If the castle was in a town, the wall ditches were filled up, and so the town was able to expand. Only the dark boulevards remind us by their names of the old martial bulwarks. The stronghold is near its decline, and comes to be used generally as a storehouse, a prison, or an outhouse, although in many cases it is protected by schemes for the care of monuments, or is renovated and established as a museum.

The strongholds situated on mountain heights were never attacked by cannon and therefore the reinforcement with bastions was not so necessary as in the defence system of the plains and around the towns. When the lord had no interest in restoration, nor the means to carry it out, the proud castle fell derelict, and only the ghosts of long-dead defenders now seem to walk the ruined battlements.

LIST OF ILLUSTRATIONS

List of Illustrations

SELECT BIBLIOGRAPHY

ANDREWS, K., Castles of the Morea, Princeton, New Jersey 1953

BOEHLAU & SCHEFOLD, Larisa am Hermos I, Die Bauten, Berlin 1940

BORCHARDT, L., Altägyptische Festungen an der zweiten Nilschwelle, Leipzig 1923

BRAUN, H., The English Castle, London 1936

Die Burgen und Schlösser der Schweiz. Hg. v. E. Probst, Basel 1929 f.

CAGNAT, R., La frontière militaire de la Tripolitaine â l'époque romaine. Mém. de l'acad. des inscr. Paris 1914

Castelos medievais de Portugal, 1949

Le Château Espagnol du Moyen Age, Madrid 1949

FEDDEN, R. - THOMSON, J., Crusader Castles, London 1957

FISCHER, G., Norske kongeborger, Oslo 1951

GALLOTTI, J., Le palais des papes, Paris 1949

HAJDUCH, J., Slovenské hrady, 1955

HARVEY, A., The castles and walled towns of England, London 1925

HASELOFF, A., Die Bauten der Hohenstaufen in Unteritalien, Leipzig 1920

HEMPEL, E., Geschichte der deutschen Baukunst, Munich 1956

LEASK, H. G., Irish Castles, Dundalk 1946

LEMAITRE, H., Châteaux en France, Paris 1948

LUKOMSKIJ, G., Alt-Rußland. Architektur und Kunstgewerbe, Munich 1923

Magyar épitészet (Ungarische Architektur bis zum Ende des XIX. Jahrhunderts), Budapest 1954

MATZ, Fr., Kreta, Mykene, Troja. Stuttgart 1956

MOES, E. W. - SLUYTERMAN, K., Nederlandsche Kasteelen en hun historie I—III, Amsterdam 1912—1915

MYLONAS, GEORGE E., Ancient Mycenae. The Capital City of Agamemnon, Princeton, N. J. 1957

O'NEIL, B. H. St. J., Castles, London 1953

NISPEN TOT SEVENAER, E. O. M. VAN, Nederlandsche Kasteelen, Amsterdam 1949

NORLUND, P., Trelleborg, Kopenhagen 1949

ROUSSELL, A., Danmarks Middelalderborge, Kopenhagen 1942

TOY, S., A history of fortification, London 1955

TUULSE, A., Borgar i Västerlandet, Stockholm 1952

Verzeichnis österreichischer Burgen und Schlösser, Vienna 1955

WEBB, G., Architecture in Britain. The middle ages, Harmonsworth 1956

WIRTH, Z., - BENDA, J., Burgen und Schlösser der Tschechoslowakei, Prague 1954

SOURCES OF ILLUSTRATIONS

LINE DRAWINGS. ARCH. L. BAKALOWITS REDREW THE LINE ILLUSTRATIONS FROM ORIGINALS IN THE FOLLOWING
WORKS: K. Andrews, Castles of the Morea: 240 — L. Bruhns, Hohenstaufenschlösser: 91, 92 — R. E. Brünnow-
Domaszewski, A. v., Die Provincia Arabia: 9 — R. Cagnat, La frontière militaire de la Tripolitaine à l'époque
romaine. Mém. de l'acad. des inscr.: 8 — Geo. T. Clark, Medieval military architecture in England I: 36, 37 —
B. Ebhardt, Deutsche Burgen: 147; Die Burgen Italiens: 87, 219; Der Wehrbau Europas im Mittelalter I: 48, 96,
98, 99, 100, 118, 144, 145, 146, 163, 164, 222, 223 — G. Eimer, topogr. photo: 86 — C. Enlart, Manuel d'archéologie
française depuis les temps Mérovingiens jusqu'à la renaissance. Architecture civile et militaire, I—II: 101 —
A. v. Essenwein, Die Kriegsbaukunst. Handbuch der Architektur, Zweiter Teil, 4. Bd., 1. H.: 43, 44, 45, 46, 60 —
G. Fischer, Norske kongeborger: 211 — A. Goldschmidt, Die normannischen Königspaläste in Palermo: 41, 42 —
A. Haseloff, Die Bauten der Hohenstaufen in Unteritalien: 88, 89, 90, 93 — U. Hoelscher, Das hohe Tor von Medinet
Habu: 1; Die Kaiserpfalz Goslar: 49 — W. Hotz, Staufische Reichsburgen am Mittelrhein: 61, 62, 63 —
R. Koldewey, Das wiedererstehende Babylon: 2 — V. V. Kostotschky, Krepostj Ivangorod: 210 — Erik B. Lundberg,
Visborgs slott. Antikvariska studier IV: 217 — Marjorie & C. H. B. Quennell, Everyday life in Anglo-Saxon,
Viking and Norman times: 32 — A. V. Millingen, Byzantine Constantinople: 67 — George E. Mylonas, Ancient
Mycenae. The Capital City of Agamemnon: 3 — B. H. St. J. O'Neil, Castles: 13, 34, 38, 221 — E. O. M. van Nispen
tot Sevenaer, Nederlandsche kasteelen: 186 — P. Nörlund, Trelleborg: 65 — M. Olsson, Kalmar slotts historia I:
212 — A. v. Oppermann & C. Schuchhardt, Atlas vorgeschichtlicher Befestigungen in Niedersachsen: 15, 16,
47 — Österreichische Kunsttopographie Vol. VIII: 175 — O. Piper, Burgenkunde: 39, 40 — E. Poeschel, Das
Burgenbuch von Graubünden: 177 — A. Raquenet, Petits artifices historiques: 18 — Rauch (G. Rodenwaldt,
Neue deutsche Ausgrabungen): 14 — J. G. N. Renaud, De bouwgeschiedenis van het Muiderslot. Bulletin van
de Kon. Ned. Oudheidkundige: 187; De Borg te Wedde: 188 — G. Rey, Etude sur les monuments de l'architecture
militaire des croisés en Syrie et dans l'ile de Chypre: 68, 69, 70, 71, 72 — Royal Commission on Ancient and
Historical Monuments of Scotland. Dumfries: 143 — Royal Commission on Historical Monuments (England).
Essex: 33, 35 — J. Sauvaget, Les ruines omeyyades du Djebel Seis. Syria 20: 12 — O. Schürer, Die Kaiserpfalz in
Eger: 59 — C. M. Smidt, Aerkebiskop Eskils Borganlaeg paa Söborg: 66; Nordsjaellands middelalderlige Mindes-
maerker. Frederiksborg Amts historiske Samfunds Aarbog: 218 — C. Steinbrecht, Preußen zur Zeit der Land-
meister: 199, 200 — O. Stiehl, Der Wohnbau des Mittelalters, Handbuch der Architektur. Zweiter Teil, Vol. 4:
64 — J. Strzygowski, Mschatta II. Jahrbuch der Königlich Preußischen Kunstsammlungen, Vol. 25: 10, 11 —
S. Toy, Castles: 17, 19, 125, 126, 127 — E. Varjù, Magyar várak: 239 — E. Viollet-le-Duc, Dictionnaire raisonné
de l'architecture française du 11e au 16e siècle: 20, 94, 95, 97, 116, 117, 220 — J. Weingartner, Bozner Burgen:
174, 176; Tiroler Burgenkunde: 224. Ill. 33, 35 with permission of the Controller of Her Majesty's Stationary office.
HALF-TONE REPRODUKTIONS. Aero-Bild-Verlag, Fulda-Bronzell: 154 — D. Anderson S. A., Rom: 79 — Ivar
Anderson, Antikvarist-topografiska arkivet: 214, 216 — Federico Arborio Mella, Milan: 124 — Schroll-Verlag,
Vienna: 7 — Archivio fotografico dell'E. P. T. di Bari: 81 — Hallam Ashley, New Costessey: 135 — Assessorato
per il Turismo della Regione Siciliana, Palermo: 30 — Hugo Atzwanger, Bozen: 170 — Lala Aufsberg, Sonthofen
im Allgäu: 57, 77, 78, 82, 150, 155 — Ernst Baumann, Bad Reichenhall: 229, 230 — Bildarchiv Deutsche Burgen
(Herbert Römer, Braubach a. Rh.): 148, 152, 156, 159 — Bildarchiv Foto Marburg: 50, 52, 53, 54, 55, 56, 104,
109, 113, 151, 153, 161, 201, 202, 204, 205, 206, 207, 208, 209, 237 — Bildarchiv der Österr. Nationalbibliothek, Vienna:
166, 168, 173 — Bord Failte Eireann, Dublin: 140, 142 — Burgenarchiv der Niederösterr. Landesregierung,
Vienna: 165, 172 — Centralna Agencja Fotograficzna, Warsaw: 228 — Prof. Dr. K.-H. Clasen, Berlin: 203 —
Commissariat Général au Tourisme de Belgique, Brussels: 196, 197, 198 — Dr. Heinrich Decker, Ostermiething:
31, 80, 84 — Deutsches Archäologisches Institut, Athens: 5, 74 — Deutsche Zentrale für Fremdenverkehr,
Frankfurt/M.: 149, 160 — Direction Générale du Tourisme (Commissariat Général au Tourisme), Paris: 22, 24,
102, 103, 105, 106, 107, 108, 110, 111, 114, 115, 227 — Dr. Gerhard Eimer, Stockholm: 112 — Ente Provinciale
per il Turismo, Parma: 85 — Antonio Ferrugento Gonçalves, Lisbon: 123 — Kunstanstalt Wilhelm Gerling sen.,
Darmstadt: 162 — Heinrich Iffland (Finska turistföreningen), Helsinki: 238 — Dr. Ing. Georg Innerebner, Bozen:
167, 169 — Istituto di Archeologia, Università di Catania: 83 — A. F. Kersting, London: 28, 129 — Nils Lagergren,
Stockholm: 215 — Landesdenkmalamt Westfalen, Münster: 158 — Landeskonservator Rheinland, Bonn: 157 —
Lichtbeelden Instituut (C. P. L. I.), Amsterdam: 189 — Foto Mas, Barcelona: 119, 120, 121, 122 — Ministerium
für Bauwesen, Denkmalamt, Budapest: 232, 233 — Ministry of Works, Edinburgh: 138 — National Buildings
Record, London: 25, 26, 27, 29, 128, 130, 131, 133, 134 — Neubacher, vorm. Bruno Reifenstein, Vienna: 171, 231 —

INDEX